Building on
Living
Stones

Building on
Living
Stones

New Testament Patterns
and Principles of Renewal

Michael Gleason

kregel
PUBLICATIONS

Grand Rapids, MI 49501

Building on Living Stones: New Testament Patterns and Principles of Renewal

Published by Kregel Publications, a division of Kregel, Inc., P.O. Box 2607, Grand Rapids, MI 49501. Kregel Publications provides trusted, biblical publications for Christian growth and service. Your comments and suggestions are valued.

Cover photo: Superstock
Cover design: Alan G. Hartman
Book design: Nicholas G. Richardson

Library of Congress Cataloging-in-Publication Data
Gleason, Michael, 1953–
  Building on living stones: New Testament patterns and principles of renewal / Michael Gleason.
      p.   cm.
  Includes bibliographical references.
      1. Church renewal. 2. Church renewal—Biblical teaching. 3. Bible. N.T.—Theology. 4. Evangelicalism—United States. I. Title.
  BV600.2.G545   1996   269—dc20   95-38412
                                             CIP

ISBN 0-8254-2729-0

Printed in the United States of America
1 2 3 4 5 / 00 99 98 97 96

For the generous support of my wife, Shelia;
the visionary service of the members, friends, and staff
of Park Street Brethren Church; and the encouragement
and editorial suggestions of Dr. Ben Witherington III
and the fine staff at Kregel Publications,
I am deeply grateful.

*Now to him who is able to do immeasurably more than
all we ask or imagine, according to his power
that is at work within us, to him be glory
in the church and in Christ Jesus throughout
all generations, for ever and ever! Amen.*
                                   Ephesians 3:20–21

CONTENTS

INTRODUCTION

I wrote this book while I served as pastor of evangelism and discipleship at an evangelical church in Ashland, Ohio. This fellowship averages, at the time of this writing, approximately 350 in Sunday attendance. The church is comprised primarily of white-collar professionals. During the academic year, students from a neighboring university and theological seminary join the church for worship.

I began the research for and the writing of this book in deep frustration. During a decade of ministry, I had launched a variety of renewal and outreach programs. In each situation I experienced more disappointment than success. My personal discouragement pressed me beyond the dozens of outreach and renewal programs that littered my bookshelves to the pages of Scripture. The goal of this search was to understand the biblical principles of renewal that operated during the great awakening of the first century. The Scripture study that followed was detailed—and liberating.

I chose for my study the New Testament books that deal with the birth and doctrine of the early church. I carefully examined the books of Acts through Jude and categorized each text that deals with evangelism or discipleship. These selected passages were then indexed on charts; one hundred typed pages was the result! The Scriptures recorded on the charts were collated until nine biblical principles of renewal emerged.

At this point my ministry changed. I was deeply impressed by the fact that renewal and evangelism in the New Testament were diverse and need-centered. I had focused on launching the latest programs hoping that the needs of people would be met and hearts would be won for Christ. The biblical model, however, turns the tables. It creates ministry strategies *in response* to the needs of those the church wants to reach. Outreach in the New Testament was people-centered rather than program-centered. In keeping with this biblical model, a group from our church surveyed community leaders to determine the unmet needs of the people in our town. This resulted in exciting fruit as various outreach ministries and support groups grew out of people's real needs.

The chapters of this book that deal with renewal through small groups and through Sunday school are unique because they encourage participants to develop a diversity of structures and ministries that are best suited to their unique situations. Our church found this approach refreshing and I believe other congregations will as well.

It will help to define a few commonly used terms. *Evangelism* will be defined as the act or process of communicating the saving message of the Gospel of Jesus Christ through words and actions. *Discipleship* will refer to the act or process of spiritual encouragement or instruction within the body of Christ. *Renewal* characterizes the process of restoration to an original or intended state. In the framework of church renewal, this is a call to return the church to a disciplined practice of evangelism and discipleship, utilizing strategies appropriate to particular cultural and ministry settings.

As an overview: Part One is a thorough examination of

nine biblical principles of renewal evident in Acts and the Epistles. These nine principles establish a broad, biblical framework out of which a variety of particular ministry patterns can be developed. The research is intentionally comprehensive and reflects a conservative view of Scripture. Part Two illustrates the development and implementation of assorted contemporary patterns of church renewal in the form of practical manuals, each of which is faithful to the nine principles. These manuals are designed to equip the professional and the lay minister for active service. Renewal through small groups, various support groups and outreach ministries, and the adult Sunday school are considered. As the manuals and appendixes are utilized, it should be with the understanding that they can be adapted to the particular ministry situation in which you are serving.

Apart from God's sovereign blessing and sustaining grace, the renewal patterns outlined in this book are nothing more than respectable group-dynamic theory clothed in Christian terms. Lasting personal renewal and spiritual change is the result of God's sovereign influence accompanied by our prayer and works of obedient service. "Faith by itself," says James, "if it is not accompanied by action, is dead" (James 2:17). We need faith and works, prayer and programs, dependency and strategy—at the same time. This is the biblical balance.

Without exception I affirm that strong organization and programming is vital to church renewal. Yet I am equally convinced that strategy without dependency, works without faith, and programs without prayer will have little significant impact for the kingdom of Christ.

PART ONE

Biblical Principles of Renewal

Chapter One

PRINCIPLES OF EVANGELISM IN ACTS

R ichard Baxter, an outstanding pastor, evangelist, and writer in the seventeenth century, presented these challenging words in *The Reformed Pastor:* "The work of conversion is the first and great thing we must drive at; after this we must labor with all our might!"[1] Without a doubt the vibrant body of believers who gathered as the first-century church in Jerusalem would have echoed a hearty amen to those words. Evangelism was one of the visible priorities of the early Christians. In a matter of months the church grew from a few hundred to many thousands. The question many of us ask is, Why? What were the principles of evangelism in operation in the first-century body of Christ that caused the church to grow so explosively? I believe a close examination of Acts brings forth two principles.

> ***Principle 1:*** Evangelism and renewal are, at their foundations, sovereign works of the triune God. The church's response is to maintain an attitude of dependency in prayer and in works of obedient service.

1. Richard Baxter, *The Reformed Pastor* (Edinburgh: Banner of Truth Trust, 1983), 94.

Jesus Christ called the church early in its formation to dependent obedience through His words in Acts 1:8: "You will receive power when the Holy Spirit comes on you; and you will be my witnesses in Jerusalem, and in all Judea and Samaria, and to the ends of the earth." Without the sovereign ministry of the Holy Spirit there is clearly no power in witnessing. In fact, the early disciples were instructed not to even attempt evangelism until they had been "clothed with power from on high" (Luke 24:49). Acts provides multiple illustrations of the work accomplished by the Spirit through an obedient, dependent, praying community of faith. There is not a ministry or task that is not dependent upon His power. The following Scripture references from Acts illustrate the central role of the Holy Spirit in the ministry of the early church.

- inspires the Scriptures (1:2,16; 28:25);
- equips people for evangelism or mission (1:5, 8; 2:4,17–18, 33; 4:8, 31; 8:29; 10:19–20; 11:12; 16:6–10; 20:22–23);
- empowers people for a specific task, ministry, or action (6:3–5; 7:55; 8:39; 10:38; 13:2–4, 9; 15:28; 20:28; 21:11);
- brings conviction of sin (5:3, 9; 7:51; 10:44);
- fills believers (2:38; 5:32; 8:15–17; 9:17; 10:45–47; 11:15–16; 15:8; 19:1–6);
- strengthens and encourages the church (9:31).

The work of the Spirit is mentioned no less than fifty-one times in Acts. In fact, it has been suggested that this book of early church missions be renamed the "Acts of the Spirit"—a fitting title indeed!

No less impressive are the recurring references to the fervent, dependent prayer that embellished the obedient church. This priority of prayer was by holy design. The compelling command in Acts 1:8 makes it clear that our Lord assigned this small but zealous body the task of world evangelism: "You will be my witnesses in Jerusalem, and in all Judea and Samaria, and to the ends of the earth." This is an impossible command! They lacked a budget, a church planting manual, and seminary degrees; they did not even have a denomination to support them! All they had was God and the supportive Christian body that surrounded them. They were pressed, in obedience, to resort to the one tool they did possess—dependent prayer. The Scripture says: "They all joined together constantly in prayer" (Acts 1:14).

What did they discover? They discovered their God to be more than adequate to accomplish this impossible task—through them! In fact, the twenty-eight chapters of this exciting record reveal the reassuring truth that God never gives the church a task to perform that He is not planning to empower it and equip it to fulfill. *He* became its power, strength, and provision. It is no wonder that the growth was so explosive and the body was so dependent. Acts contains at least the following twenty-four references to prayer: 1:14, 24; 2:42; 4:31; 6:4, 6; 8:15; 9:11, 40; 10:2–4, 9, 30–31; 11:5; 12:5, 12; 13:3; 14:23; 16:13, 16, 25; 20:36; 21:5; 22:17; 28:8.

> ***Principle 2:*** The New Testament church used a variety of evangelistic activities and methods. Most were chosen to meet the specific physical, spiritual, or emotional needs of the individuals or groups it was attempting to reach. The evangelism was people-centered rather than program-centered.

Evangelism in Acts was clearly diverse and often need-centered. It was not always proclamational (Acts 2:44–47), yet at times it was solely proclamational (2:14–41). It was a miraculous healing that graced a social outcast, drawing a crowd of thousands to hear the Gospel (3:2–26). Evangelism took place when a bold disciple addressed an angry mob in uncompromising terms (Acts 7) and when his friend quietly shared his faith with an Ethiopian eunuch (8:26–39). It occurred as a single event on the road to Damascus (9:1–18) and through a deepening relationship over several years with Felix the governor (Acts 24). Evangelism was accompanied by tongues of fire (2:1–12) and was spread through the death of a martyr (7:54–8:4). Evangelism occurred when Tabitha was raised from the dead, an event that stirred a town to conviction (9:36–42). It was in the hymns of imprisoned disciples and in forgiveness experienced by a destitute jailer (Acts 16:16–34). Evangelism took place as the hand of God worked in diverse ways to touch parched and broken lives.

A closer look at the first five chapters of Acts will further illustrate this principle. The diversity in the Spirit-inspired methodologies and in the need-centered approaches to ministry are evident.

Text	Need	Method	Result
2:1–12	The crowd spoke different languages.	The believers spoke foreign languages.	All heard the Gospel in their own tongues.
2:44–47	People had practical and relational needs.	Practical ministries.	Believers enjoyed favor with all the people; many were saved.

Text	Need	Method	Result
3:2–4:4	A man was unable to walk.	Peter healed him.	A crowd gathered; Peter proclaimed the Gospel.
5:12–16	People were sick and tormented.	Signs, wonders, healing.	Crowds came to the apostles.
5:17–42	The Sadducees did not believe in resurrection or in afterlife.	Deliverance of the apostles from jail.	The apostles declared the resurrection and glorification of Christ.

The following references in Acts include all the remaining evangelistic encounters and accompanying Spirit-inspired methodologies, which will shed additional light on this principle for the reader who would like to pursue this theme in greater detail:

no method mentioned (6:7; 9:31; 11:22–24; 12:24);
signs, wonders, and proclamations (6:8–10; 14:3–7);
preaching or proclamation (7:1–8:4; 8:25; 9:19–22; 10:22–48; 13:14–49; 14:1, 21, 25; 17:10–12, 18–34; 18:5–8; 19:8–9; 26:1–29; 28:31);
signs, exorcism, healing, and proclamation (8:5–12; 19:11–20);
discussion (8:26–38; 9:28–30; 16:13–15; 17:2–5, 16–17; 18:4, 19–21, 24–26, 28; 28:23–24);

direct encounter with the risen Christ (9:1–18);
healing (9:34–35);
proclamation and confrontation (13:6–12);
raising a dead person to life (9:36–42);
persecution and proclamation (8:1–4, 11:19–21,
      21:27–22:22; 22:30–23:11; 24:1–27);
healing and proclamation (14:8–17);
exorcism, persecution, miraculous deliverance,
      and proclamation (16:16–34).

What can be deduced from a thorough examination of
the evangelistic methodology in Acts? In simple terms
neither Acts nor the rest of the New Testament develops
an inclusive program for evangelism. In fact, quite the
opposite is true. The physical, spiritual, emotional, and
cultural needs of the non-Christian community inspired
diverse methods. To put it another way, the church
functioned as a living organism, not as a rigid, closed
organization; it was people-centered rather than program-
centered.

Chapter Two

PRINCIPLES OF EVANGELISM IN THE EPISTLES

T he Epistles are instructional letters to the growing church and its leaders. In most of the letters, particularly those written by Paul, there are multiple testimonies of the authors' personal evangelistic ministries or burdens. Many also contain specific outlines of the Gospel message (Romans, for example) that could be considered evangelistic if read in the hearing of a non-Christian audience. Comparatively few, however, are the instructional passages that focus specifically on evangelism. But examination of these passages yields four more principles of evangelism.

> ***Principle 3:*** There is a New Testament gift of evangelism.

The gift of evangelism is mentioned only three times in the New Testament. In Acts 21:8, Philip is called "the evangelist." Ephesians 4:11 places the gift alongside other gifts that equip the church. In 2 Timothy 4:5, Timothy is exhorted to "do the work of an evangelist." From these passages, we conclude that the gift of evangelism is an operational gift of the Spirit. This gift is a function of certain members of the body, like Philip and Timothy, given to equip God's people for works of service (Eph. 4:11–12). The church must provide opportunities of service and leadership whereby the gift might be exercised.

> **Principle 4:** Lifestyle evangelism is basic to proclamational evangelism.

Lifestyle evangelism is the thrust of a majority of the instructional passages on evangelism. The two passages that provide specific instructions for proclamational evangelism, Colossians 4:6 and 1 Peter 3:15, are found in the context of lifestyle exhortations. For example, Colossians 4:6 states: "Let your conversation be always full of grace, seasoned with salt, so that you may know how to answer everyone." Just before this, in verse 5, Paul exhorts the church to "be wise in the way you act toward outsiders, making the most of every opportunity."

I believe the primary conclusion to be drawn from this principle is that lifestyle is essential to witness. The gospel of love and forgiveness usually finds increased response when accompanied by corresponding acts of charity and mercy. Simply stated: Christians should practice what they preach. The following instructions exhort the entire church to practice a lifestyle and a proclamational witness.

Lifestyle Evangelism
Romans 12:17–21: Do not repay anyone evil for evil. Be careful to do what is right in the eyes of everybody. . . . Live at peace with everyone. Do not take revenge.
Romans 13:8–10: Let no debt remain outstanding, except the continuing debt to love one another. . . . Love does no harm to its neighbor.
1 Corinthians 10:32–33: Do not cause anyone to stumble, . . . even as I try to please everybody in every way.

For I am not seeking my own good but the good of many, so that they may be saved.

Galatians 6:10: Therefore, as we have opportunity, let us do good to all people.

Colossians 4:5: Be wise in the way you act toward outsiders; make the most of every opportunity.

1 Thessalonians 4:11–12: Lead a quiet life, . . . mind your own business, . . . work with your hands . . . so that your daily life may win the respect of outsiders.

1 Timothy 6:1: All who are under the yoke of slavery should consider their [unbelieving] masters worthy of full respect, so that God's name and our teaching may not be slandered.

Titus 2:9–10: Teach slaves to be subject to their masters in everything, to try to please them, not to talk back to them, and not to steal from them, but show that they can be fully trusted, so that in every way they will make the teaching about God our Savior attractive.

1 Peter 2:12: Live such good lives among the pagans that . . . they may see your good deeds and glorify God on the day he visits us.

1 Peter 3:1–2: Wives . . . be submissive to your husbands so that, if any of them do not believe the word, they may be won over without words by the behavior of their wives.

1 Peter 3:16: . . . keeping a clear conscience, so that those who speak maliciously against your good behavior in Christ may be ashamed of their slander.

Proclamational Evangelism

Colossians 4:6: Let your conversation be always full of grace, seasoned with salt, so that you may know how to answer everyone.

1 Peter 3:15: Always be prepared to give an answer to

everyone who asks you to give the reason for the hope that you have. But do this with gentleness and respect."

> ***Principle 5:*** Every member of the church is expected to evangelize.

Paul and Peter intended the entire reading audience, not just those with the gift of evangelism, to fulfill the instructions. Teachings on lifestyle, and in some cases proclamational, evangelism in the Epistles are addressed to the total church in Rome, in Corinth, in Galatia, in Colosse, in Thessalonica, and to the "strangers in the world, scattered throughout Pontus, Galatia, Cappadocia, Asia, and Bithynia" (1 Pet. 1:1). We know that the church was born in missionary fervor so most early believers were no doubt zealous to evangelize. Although we are separated by centuries from them, evangelism is no less the imperative commission of the church today.

> ***Principle 6:*** Leaders are exhorted to model evangelism and a consistent Christian lifestyle.

Several Scripture passages exhort leaders to model evangelism and a consistent Christian lifestyle. First Timothy 3:2–12 deals specifically with the task of an overseer. Paul commissions those who occupy this position to "have a good reputation with outsiders" (v. 7). The counsel in Titus 1:6–9 is directed to elders and instructs that "an elder must be blameless, the husband of but one wife, a man whose children believe" (v. 6). In the other related teaching, 2 Timothy 4:5, Paul encourages his disciple to "do the work of an evangelist."

Additional lifestyle expectations for leadership are outlined in 1 Timothy 3:2–6, 8–10,12, and in Titus 1:6–9.

Elder/Overseer
- above reproach
- husband of one wife
- temperate
- self-controlled
- respectable
- hospitable
- able to teach
- not given to drunkenness
- not violent
- gentle
- not a lover of money
- manages his family well
- sees that his children obey and respect him
- not a recent convert
- blameless
- has believing children
- not overbearing
- not quick-tempered
- does not pursue dishonest gain
- lover of good
- upright
- holy
- disciplined
- holds firmly to sound doctrine

Deacon
- worthy of respect
- sincere
- does not indulge in much wine
- does not pursue dishonest gain
- holds to the deep truths of the faith
- maintains a clear conscience
- husband of one wife
- manages his children and household well

One can conclude from these Scripture passages that leaders are exhorted to model, at home and in the world, evangelism that is accompanied by a consistent Christian lifestyle. It is obvious that neither evangelism nor a Christian lifestyle is expected only of those who lead; however, it is often the leaders who encourage and maintain these disciplines in the body of Christ through, among other avenues, consistent modeling. In the words of Peter: "Be shepherds of God's flock that is under your care, serving as overseers . . . being *examples* to the flock" (1 Pet. 5:2–3, emphasis mine).

Chapter Three

PRINCIPLES OF DISCIPLESHIP IN ACTS AND THE EPISTLES

A round A.D. 50, the apostle Paul sent a letter to the *ekklesia,* or "church," of the Thessalonians. Scholars believe this use of *ekklesia* in 1 Thessalonians 1:1 is the first use of this word in a New Testament writing. Paul and other New Testament writers freely applied this term in a variety of contexts. For example, in Philemon 2 and in Colossians 4:15 Paul describes the *ekklesia* as a gathering of Christians who meet in a home. Paul again addresses the *ekklesia* in 1 Corinthians 11:18 and 14:19 in the much larger context of a public worship service. In Romans 16:16, Galatians 1:2, 1 Thessalonians 1:1, and 2 Thessalonians 1:1, the word has a pluralistic sense; each letter includes in its address all of the particular churches in the city that may be reading the letter at one time or another. The word is broadened further to include the universal church in such passages as 1 Corinthians 11:16, Galatians 1:13, and Philippians 3:6. In Acts, *ekklesia* is used several ways: as referring to one gathered body, 5:11 and 14:27; in a pluralistic sense describing all the area churches, 9:31; and finally to describe even a secular assembly called out for business purposes, 19:39–41.

The word *ekklesia*, however, is never used in reference to a building. The church of the New Testament was always an assembly of *people.* These people gathered as a family, a holy assembly, the very body of Christ! And the living Lord Jesus Christ was in their midst.

The New Testament is a careful record of specific guidelines for spiritual encouragement and instruction in the body of Christ. Three principles of discipleship emerge from this record.

> **Principle 1:** Members of the body of Christ are dependent on and accountable to one another.

The New Testament is clear that the body of Christ is inseparably joined in the fullness of *koinonia,* a Greek word for "fellowship" that is frequently used and frequently misunderstood. The word is derived from *koinos* which means "'common' (a) in the sense of common ownership, property, ideas, etc., (b) in the sense of what concerns all, e.g., societies, monies, resolves."[2] *Koinonia* in the New Testament means a joint participation in all of life, as was evidenced in the early assembly by those who "had everything in common" (Acts 2:44). Perhaps one of the greatest pictures of the intimacy authentic *koinonia* demands is found in the words of Romans 12:5. "So in Christ we who are many form one body, and *each member belongs to all the others"* (emphasis mine). We are "in Christ"; that means He now owns us! Gone is the rugged American individualism for those who meet as the *ekklesia* of Jesus Christ—no more mine and yours; in Christ all now becomes ours and His.

Clearly, the members of the church are dependent on and accountable to, each other. Mutual edification is experienced through shared ministry and *koinonia,* two

---

2. Gerhard Kittel and Gerhard Friedrich, eds., *Theological Dictionary of the New Testament,* trans. Geoffrey W. Bromiley, abridged in one vol. (Grand Rapids: Eerdmans, 1985), 447.

themes richly rooted in the New Testament. The following categories of shared ministry and *koinonia* illustrate
the interdependence and mutual accountability God desires the body of Christ to experience.

The body of Christ
  has "everything in common" (Acts 2:44–47; 4:32);
  shares financial burdens (Acts 11:29–30; Rom.
      12:13; 15:26; 2 Cor. 8:2; Phil. 4:15);
  shares the suffering of its members (Acts 12:5; 2
      Cor. 1:5–7; Phil. 1:7; Col. 1:24; Heb. 10:33–
      34);
  shares ministry functions (Rom. 12:4–8; 1 Cor. 12–
      14; Eph. 4:11–16; 1 Pet. 4:10–11);
  shares the sacraments (Matt. 26:26–28; 28:19; Acts
      2:41; 8:12; 9:18; 1 Cor. 11:17–34);
  is governed by gifted, qualified, and divinely ap-
      pointed leaders (Acts 14:23; 1 Tim. 3:1–13;
      Titus 1:5–9; Eph. 4:11–12; 1 Pet. 5:1–4);
  encourages strong family life (1 Tim. 3:2, 4–5,12;
      Titus 1:6; Eph. 5:21–6:4; Col. 3:18–21; 1 Pet.
      3:1–7);
  shares a ministry of prayer (Acts 2:42; 12:5; Rom.
      1:9–10; 12:12; 15:30–31; Col. 4:2–4; 1 Pet. 4:7;
      Eph. 6:18–20);
  is involved in "one another" ministry:
      Romans 12:10: Be devoted to one another in
          brotherly love. Honor one another above
          yourselves.
      Romans 12:16: Live in harmony with one
          another.
      Romans 13:8: Love one another.
      Romans 14:13: Stop passing judgment on one
          another.
      Romans 15:7: Accept one another.

Romans 15:14: Instruct one another.

1 Corinthians 12:25: Have equal concern for each other.

Galatians 5:13: Serve one another in love.

Galatians 5:15: If you keep on biting and devouring each other, watch out or you will be destroyed by each other.

Galatians 6:2: Carry each other's burdens.

Ephesians 4:2: . . . bearing with one another in love.

Ephesians 4:32: Be kind and compassionate to one another, forgiving each other.

Ephesians 5:19: Speak to one another with psalms, hymns and spiritual songs.

Ephesians 5:21: Submit to one another.

Colossians 3:13: Bear with each other and forgive whatever grievances you may have against one another.

Hebrews 10:24–25: Spur one another on toward love and good deeds. Encourage one another.

James 4:11: Do not slander one another.

James 5:9: Don't grumble against each other.

James 5:16: Confess your sins to each other and pray for each other so that you may be healed.

1 Peter 1:22: Love one another deeply, from the heart.

1 Peter 4:8–9: Above all, love each other deeply. . . . Offer hospitality to one other without grumbling.

1 Peter 5:5: Clothe yourselves with humility toward one another.

1 Peter 5:14: Greet one another with a kiss of love.

1 John 3:11, 23, 4:7, 11, 12; 2 John 5: Love one another.

> **Principle 2:** Small groups are often used by the Holy Spirit to initiate and to sustain discipleship in the body.

Members of the body of Christ are indeed intended to be interdependent and accountable. This principle, if taken seriously, raises several fundamental questions that need to be addressed to contemporary church structure. How, for example, can a church develop shared ministry and vital *koinonia* when a majority of its members meet together for only one hour every Sunday morning? Do those church members who elect to become involved in one of the other church structures (such as Sunday school or various auxiliary groups) discover a context where finances, sufferings, gifts, burdens, compassion, confession of sins, forgiveness, encouragement, and love can be shared with honesty among the gathered *ekklesia?* Is *koinonia*, in the sense of common ownership, properties, ideas, and what concerns all actually being practiced in most of the Christian community? If not, why not?

Perhaps an answer to this question can be discovered by studying the basic structure of the *ekklesia* to which the biblical exhortations were originally addressed. What was the context of ministry that enabled Christians to readily apply much of what they learned? The early church generally gathered as small groups in the various homes of the believing community. The church was any place two or more gathered in Christ's name.

In Acts, for example, there appears to be *ekklesia* at the houses of Mary (12:12), the jailer (16:32–34), Jason (17:5–6), and Philip the Evangelist (21:8). It was to the small groups in Rome that Paul said, "Greet Priscilla and Aquila. . . . Greet also the church that meets at their house"

(Rom. 16:3–5). To the house churches in Colosse, Paul sends the following closing request: "Give my greetings to the brothers at Laodicea, and to Nympha and the church in her house" (Col. 4:15). Philemon also hosted a house church (Philem. 2). In fact, New Testament scholar Wayne A. Meeks writes that "the meeting places of the Pauline groups, and probably of most other early Christian groups, were private homes."[3]

These small house churches, due to their size, informal atmosphere, and lack of time constraints, experienced the fullness of *koinonia* and active shared ministry. The small group undoubtedly enhanced their ability to be the interdependent body of Christ, mutually serving one another in love.

> ***Principle 3:*** The ministry of the Word is essential to the growth of the body.

The New Testament writers, in particular the apostle Paul, taught that the Holy Scriptures are central and essential to the growth of the body of Christ. In his timeless advice to his coworker Timothy, Paul says: "But as for you, continue in what you have learned and have become convinced of, because you know those from whom you learned it, and how from infancy you have known the Holy Scriptures, which are able to make you wise for salvation through faith in Jesus Christ." He continues, "All Scripture is God-breathed and is useful for teaching, rebuking, correcting, and training in righteousness, so that the man of God may be thoroughly equipped for every good work" (2 Tim. 3:14–17).

This passage is indeed bountiful in meaning! "All Scripture is God-breathed," the apostle declares.

---

3. Kittel, abridged in one vol., 447.

Although the original Greek is difficult to translate, either rendering of the text, "All Scripture is inspired of God," or "All Scripture, inspired of God,"[4] distinctly communicates the author's belief that the Scriptures are indeed inspired writing. No other book ever written can claim such divine authorship without being in gross error.

Paul continues to instruct Timothy concerning the content of the inspired text in verses 16 and 17 with the following thoughts: all that is essential to the growth of the body of Christ, teaching, rebuking, correcting, and training in righteousness, are "breathed" into its pages. So adequate is the Word that it produces people of God who are "thoroughly equipped for every good work." Clearly the ministry of the Word is essential to the growth of the body of Christ.

The following passages further illustrate the authoritative and central role the Word held in the life of the early church: Acts 2:42; Romans 10:14–21; 1 Thessalonians 2:13; 1 Peter 1:10–12, 23–25; 2 Peter 1:21; 3:2; and Revelation 1:2–3.

Principles of Evangelism

1. Evangelism and renewal are, at their foundations, sovereign works of the triune God. The church's response is to maintain an attitude of dependency in prayer and in works of obedient service.
2. The New Testament church used a variety of evangelistic activities and methods. Most were chosen to meet the specific physical, spiritual, or emotional needs of the individuals or groups it was attempting to reach. Evangelism was people-centered rather than program-centered.

---

4. Wayne A. Meeks, *The First Urban Christians* (New Haven: Yale University Press, 1983), 75.

3. There is a New Testament gift of evangelism.

4. Lifestyle evangelism is basic to proclamational evangelism.
5. Every member of the body of Christ is expected to evangelize.
6. Leaders are exhorted to model evangelism and a consistent Christian lifestyle.

Principles of Discipleship

1. Members of the body of Christ are dependent on, and accountable to, one another.
2. Small groups are often used by the Holy Spirit to initiate and to sustain discipleship in the body.
3. The ministry of the Word is essential to the growth of the body.

PART TWO

Contemporary Patterns of Renewal

Chapter Four

RENEWAL THROUGH SMALL GROUPS

E vangelism and discipleship experienced in the earliest days of the church are described thus:

> They devoted themselves to the apostles' teaching and to the fellowship, to the breaking of bread and to prayer. Everyone was filled with awe, and many wonders and miraculous signs were done by the apostles. All the believers were together and had everything in common. Selling their possessions and goods, they gave to anyone as he had need. Everyday they continued meeting together in the temple courts. They broke bread in their homes and ate together with glad and sincere hearts, praising God and enjoying the favor of all the people. And the Lord added to their number daily those who were being saved (Acts 2:42–47).

What is clear in this description is that evangelism and discipleship were experienced among the believers. What is not clear is all of the particular forms of evangelism and discipleship that were used. For example, we know the early believers met daily in the temple courts, but how often did they meet in small groups in their homes? How were these home meetings structured? Did they meet for one hour, two? Was there one leader or were there several? Did one person pray, or everyone? We perceive that evangelism was practiced but what were the methods? Was the evangelism centered around miraculous signs or was it mainly relational, practiced through a contagious congregation who gave to anyone as he or she had need and enjoyed the favor of all the people?

Develop

Acts clearly discloses that there were indeed not one but a variety of evangelism and discipleship activities in the early church. Present-day group ministries should also affirm diversity in the styles of evangelism and discipleship that are practiced by their small groups. In other words, not all the groups in a congregation have to be exactly alike! The only absolutes that each of the small groups at my church are asked to apply are the principles of renewal, appendix 1-A. The small-group forms and tools provided in appendix 1, as well as the insights in this chapter, were developed with this presupposition of diverse application in mind.

Inform Boards

The leadership of a church or Christian organization should be informed about the development and ongoing expansion of the small-group ministry. Mature

Change often is more warmly greeted if allowed to enter slowly.

and gifted congregation officers will often provide valuable insights for small-group leaders. This foundational procedure is also essential for their long-term support of the ministry. We found it helpful to provide printed materials for boards to review prior to a presentation so that each member had adequate time to digest the new ideas. Change often is more warmly greeted if allowed to enter slowly. The goal during the development stage is primarily to gain permission to launch a test group, not necessarily to enlist the direct participation of each board member.

Select Leaders

In characteristic simplicity, Jesus taught that "A student is not above his teacher, but everyone who is fully trained will be like his teacher" (Luke 6:40). Christ was declaring that values are both caught and taught; students act like their teachers in lifestyle, not just in thought. Indeed, one could say that a group member, or student, can be identified by the similarities in lifestyle to his or her teacher. Because the first group will provide leadership for future groups, great care and intentionality should be applied to selecting its leaders.

To aid in the selection process, a ministry guideline sheet was developed, appendix 1-D. In our church, I personally handpicked the first innovative leadership group, after much prayer for spiritual guidance, based on their gifts, maturity, and Christian lifestyle that visibly reflected the biblical standards for leadership. Often individuals with innovative personalities have the greatest desire to participate in a test group. In addition, we found it helpful to have representation from each adult Sunday school class. The Sunday school is a natural vehicle from which to launch small-group ministries. A key representative from each class helped other class members "own" the concept.

Establish Covenant

Prior to launching a small-group ministry, a group covenant should be developed that provides flexibility of form while maintaining loyalty to biblical principles. Appendix 1-B is an illustration of a covenant that incorporates these priorities. Appendix 1-C is a companion series of studies intended to assist group participants in the development of such a covenant. The biblical principles of evangelism and discipleship are built into the structure and content of each.

> ### Depend on God's sovereign work.

For example, the studies and the introductory section of the covenant promote interdependence within the body of Christ. The instructional section of the covenant and introductory study session 2 encourage an attitude of dependence upon God for His sovereign work in the renewal process. The group purpose reflects priorities of evangelism and discipleship and the group agenda and goals are intentionally flexible, allowing a variety of applications. Mutual accountability is stressed as group members agree on an attendance commitment to share-group meetings. Our small-group goals encouraged participants to make intentional, accountable decisions in the areas of outward and inward growth. Inward growth goals include a deliberate emphasis on group and personal Bible study. Outward growth goals challenge group participants to specifically target unchurched friends as well as new church attendees they desire to include in their share-group family.

It has been our observation that the groups that place a stronger emphasis on evangelistic ministry usually have a member or two who possess the gift of evangelism and accept the primary responsibility to encourage and to initiate outside contacts. When an unbelieving guest joins the group, the rest of the members assume the integral role of sharing Christ's love through their lives, unique gifts, and timely words.

Test

The initial group will require approximately nine months to test and refine the proposed small-group model. This amount of time, particularly with the original group, is most important. The climate of love and sensitivity, as well as the depth of spiritual maturity to be realized in future groups, must initially be experienced among the constituents of the test group before they can effectively transfer it.

Launch Test Group

Launching a test group is an exciting experience! The best way to establish an infant group is to involve the group members in the process of studying and completing the group covenant. This procedure provides a valuable modeling experience and solidifies the future direction of the group. During the first several sessions it is also advantageous to carefully examine the Biblical Principles of Renewal, a study that will provide a biblical foundation and a standard of measurement for future group decisions. In addition, the test group will benefit from a monthly exposure to the leadership training materials, appendix 1-E.

Quarterly evaluations of the group covenants, training materials, and study suggestions will assist the leaders in shaping these tools and materials to their particular context of ministry. At this point, pastors must provide flexibility within the boundaries of biblical principles, to allow the test group, as well as subsequent groups, the freedom to develop their own unique forms. In our particular context, for example, we developed and tested three different group covenants over a period of two years until we settled on one we felt was biblically sound and contextually acceptable.

Update Boards

Church leaders should be updated on a regular basis as to the progress and intentions of the test group. It may be helpful to have group members talk to the leadership boards several times through the year concerning the beneficial role the group plays in their own personal and spiritual journeys. Board approval should be secured prior to launching a large-scale promotion of a small-group ministry in the church.

Launch

Promote

A churchwide promotion is introduced, generally in September. It has been our experience that share-group attendees have a weighty influence over their immediate peer groups; thus, a Sunday school presentation from a share-group leader or attendee to his or her class associates has proven to be a most effective means to expand share-group interest and participation. Personal invitations as well as interviews before the congregation, appendix 1-F, have also been productive.

After the fall promotion is complete, usually a two- to three-week process, the initial share-group team is called together to review the names of interested congregation members. The requests of new registrants for participation in a specific group or with a particular leader are honored. Those who did not signify a specific group are carefully and prayerfully assigned to a group by consensus of the leaders.

Limit Group Size

The size of new groups is generally limited to about six to eight participants. This limit provides each group with enough free space to grow as they develop the outward growth goals of their share-group covenant. Often the new participants, invited to meet the outward growth goals, are unchurched friends of group members or new church attendees who were reluctant to express interest in the share group during the fall promotion. The ongoing focus on fulfilling outward growth goals, along with the initial size limitation, allows for dozens of additional individuals to be brought into the groups who did not join during the fall promotional efforts.

Hold Leaders Accountable

Group leaders meet on a regular basis with pastors and other group facilitators to give account of the personal and spiritual growth of those who are entrusted to their charge. A suggestion for the basic structure of the monthly one-hour luncheon meeting is as follows:

1. Have prayer, devotional meditation, and lunch, and discuss monthly small-group evaluations, insights, or materials, appendix 1-E. Materials are generally sent to each leader prior to the meeting.

2. Meet in clusters of three with a share-group

captain, appendix 1-G, facilitating each small group. End with specific prayer for each share-group member.

The first part of the meeting takes approximately twenty to thirty minutes. The heart of our time together, however, occurs in the clusters, where group leaders share burden and blessing with their coworkers in Christ. It is also in this context that the attendance of each group member is reported as recorded on a specific form, appendix 1-H. The share-group captain compiles all the attendance records and transfers them to a master book, appendix 1-I, where permanent records are maintained. This allows the structure to remain personal as the number of share groups grows. Every sheep is important and the growth of each is carefully monitored. The leaders conclude with specific prayer for each group and its members.

Understand the Stages of Group Life

Early in our experience with small groups, one group leader came to the monthly leaders' meeting with some startling news. Her group was experiencing some areas of contention and was seriously considering disbanding. To help the group work through this conflict stage, materials were developed and presented to all the leaders. This particular leader carefully reviewed the materials and later commented: "I didn't know that Christian groups generally experience a stage of conflict. I thought we must have been doing something wrong." The group was able to deal with their differences openly over the course of a few weeks and move on to develop plans for an extensive visitation ministry to area shut-ins. Each member experienced a renewed sense of commitment to the group and its mission.

Based on this experience, now all share groups are asked to spend a session considering these stages of group life sometime between their fourth and eighth week of meeting. This time frame allows groups to deal with potential conflict situations before they become major sources of contention (see appendix 1-J).

Courtship. Courtship takes place in the first weeks of group life. Group members may be a bit reluctant to share on a personal level because relationships are just being formed and mutual trust has not yet been established. Informal get-acquainted questions and the discipline of jointly completing the share-group covenant provide opportunities to deepen relationships and develop a common trust. For most groups, the courtship stage is an exciting and positive phase.

Conflict. The excitement of courtship will give way to the inevitable conflict that occurs, in differing degrees, when diverse personalities meet together over a period of time. For example, small groups often host overtalkers and undertalkers, who each irritate the other. In almost every group there is the wise old owl who seems to have a suggestion for every problem, along with a member who never seems free of difficulties. There are those who enjoy controversial discussions and others who will give in just to avoid conflict. Some people weep easily; others rarely show emotion.

Not every group will experience a dramatic conflict stage, but each will need to adjust to the differing personalities and perspectives that surface as a natural part of group interaction. The group will either endure or mature at this phase, based on the willingness of each individual to sincerely practice the mandates of Scripture that apply to interpersonal conflict.

Consider mandates such as: "If your brother sins against you, go and show him his fault, just between the two of you" (Matt. 18:15); "Accept him whose faith is weak without passing judgment on disputable matters. . . . Why do you judge your brother? Or why do you look down on your brother? . . . Let us therefore make every effort to do what leads to peace and to mutual edification" (Rom. 14:1, 10, 19); "Accept one another, then, just as Christ accepted you, in order to bring praise to God" (Rom. 15:7); "In your anger do not sin: Do not let the sun go down while you are still angry" (Eph. 4:26).

> *Group members soon come to accept each other, warts and all.*

To grow beyond this stage, the group must be gently guided by the various biblical mandates that encourage a sensitive balance between acceptance and confrontation. Some members who resist *any* type of conflict may even decide to leave. This phase, however, is part of the maturing process of the group and will generally resolve itself in a period of weeks. Group members soon come to accept each other, warts and all. A deeper level of trust will result and the group will start to see itself as a family. The groups who have moved through the awkwardness of this stage soon enjoy the intimacy of community—and it's worth it!

Community. Community is a peaceful stage in the life of the group. Members are relaxed and at home with one another. The attitude of mutual trust that is now felt among group members yields deeper and more personal levels of sharing. Personal ministry is occurring and inward growth is the visible fruit. Often a group needs to meet for six to nine months before the community stage is fully experienced.

In the midst of the bliss of community, however, there is a tendency for groups to focus only on inward and personal growth to the exclusion of outward growth. This is a natural desire but not a biblical one. The New Testament is clear that part of our reason for existence is to help others experience the intimate love of Christ and the supportive Christian community that those in the group have come to deeply value. In the words of Jesus: "Therefore go and make disciples of all nations" (Matt. 28:19). Those who heed this challenge discover that the degree of community they experience in ministry, inwardly and outwardly, frequently surpasses the degree of community they had previously enjoyed during their season of strictly inward growth!

It is for this reason that groups are encouraged to be sensitive to invite new individuals or families into their circle of fellowship. To further promote the growth of Christian community, groups are requested in the fall of each year either to provide leaders for new groups or to continue to openly invite others to participate in their established group.

Evaluate

We have discovered that group attendees and leaders benefit from an evaluation, which we conduct sometime in January. The evaluation sheets for group members, appendix 1-K, was designed to help participants measure themselves and their group in light of the previously established inward and outward growth goals. The leaders' evaluation, appendix 1-L, provides the opportunity for an appraisal of the monthly leaders' meeting and related materials. The evaluation sessions are often the boost that leaders and participants seem to need to maintain quality ministry.

Expand

Sow Seeds for Growth

Many group leaders indicate that it has been helpful to start sowing the seeds for growth among group members several months prior to the fall promotion. Several forms have been created to assist this seed-sowing process. One form, Two Types of Group Personalities, appendix 1-M, has been used to help group members analyze their individual contributions to the group. The two personalities outlined on this form, the "pioneer," or innovator, and the "rancher," or maintainer, often find themselves in conflict when growth and outreach are discussed. This document helps people identify each other's roles in the group as positive contributions rather than as conflicting differences.

Another form, Strategies for a Growing Family, appendix 1-N, directly applies the information in Two Types of Group Personalities. This form should be introduced in the spring and then finalized before the September

> *Plant and cultivate "missionary" seeds in the hearts of group attendees.*

share-group leaders' meeting. These materials promote discussion of growth options in anticipation of the fall promotion.

The discussion of the ideas on these forms is often accompanied by a degree of frustration and resistance. This resistance may be partially due to the fact that Americans are traditionally very private people who require a longer span of time to establish trust and openness in their relationships. Thus, they are generally reluctant to change their group structure when meaningful relationships with other group attendees have been developed. Therefore, groups are not requested to make a final decision on their particular outreach application, unless they desire to do so, until the fall promotion, when an obvious need is established. The initial presentation in the spring is intended to plant and cultivate "missionary" seeds in the hearts of group attendees.

Leaders, however, must be firm at this point to communicate to their groups that outreach is indeed essential biblically and is, without compromise, part of our group priorities. With this common understanding in mind, each group is expected to make some type of outreach application.

Plan for the Summer

Groups are requested to decide on their summer plans prior to the May leaders' meeting. At least one monthly fellowship event is encouraged through the summer. Group leaders end their monthly meetings in May and resume in August, leaving June and July free. Vacations and relaxed summer schedules have made a consistent attendance at the leaders' meetings virtually impossible. We have also observed that our leaders appreciate a break in the routine. Usually all existing groups will begin regular meetings by mid-September. Groups do not complete a group covenant, however, until after the fall promotion concludes and the new groups are established, generally around mid-October.

Recruit and Train New Leaders

All new group-leaders are prayerfully recruited prior to September, primarily through personal invitation from pastors or from incumbent share-group leaders. Spiritual gifts, maturity, and a Christian lifestyle that visibly reflects the biblical standards for leadership, as outlined in the share-group strategies, appendix 1-N, are prominent factors in the recruitment process. Each new leader is approved by consensus of the share-group leaders. Those who qualify and agree to serve are next led through a training seminar in which they examine the Biblical Principles of Renewal, the ministry guidelines, the group covenant and introductory studies, the format and importance of the monthly leaders' meetings, and basic leadership skills for facilitating a small group, appendixes 1-A through 1-E.

Promote

Each September, plans are launched to again promote the share-group ministry (see appendix 1-F for related materials). About this time groups meet to finalize decisions for growth using the Strategies for a Growing Family. The group leader plays a central role in motivating group members to develop a strategy for the growing share-group family. Many of our groups experience a fresh excitement and new vision for growth during this season of reflection. The groups wrestle with their own particular outreach applications for one or two sessions. Each group is asked to make some type of outreach application, even if it is different from the options listed. Pastors are available to visit groups and help them through their decision-making process.

After the promotion is completed, usually a two- to three-week process, the group leaders meet to review the names of congregation members who indicated their interest in share groups, as well as the particular strategy chosen by each share group to help incorporate the new

registrants. A master list is then created of the new registrants, which in turn determines the required number of
new groups and leaders. Requests to participate in a specific group are honored. Those who did not specify a
group are carefully and prayerfully assigned to new or
established groups by consensus of the leaders. New
members who are to be invited into established groups
are expected to be contacted by mid-October. New groups
should be underway by about that time as well.

Chapter Five

RENEWAL THROUGH SUPPORT GROUPS AND OUTREACH MINISTRIES

T he New Testament church utilized a variety of evangelistic activities and methods. Most were chosen
by the church to meet the specific physical, spiritual, or
emotional needs of the individuals or groups it was
attempting to reach. Evangelism was therefore people-
centered rather than program-centered. The development
of this biblical principle in contemporary ministry can
be equally diverse. The multiple human needs and broken
lives that are found in every community provide the
church with vast opportunities for service through
support groups and outreach ministries.

Research

In order to establish effective support groups and outreach ministries, the actual needs that exist in a given
community must be discerned before specific groups or
ministries are developed. When attempting to discern the
community needs, interested church leaders and layper-
sons will find an invaluable resource in the professionals in the various government or private community

service agencies, funeral homes, counseling centers, nursing homes, and so forth. Appointments should be made with these professionals with the goal of inviting them to identify, from their perspectives, the needs among the people who live in the community. Insights should also be gleaned from what they suggest as effective means of serving people in identified need groups.

> *God is the one who calls workers into ministry.*

Early in the formation of our support groups and outreach ministries, several in our fellowship followed this course of action. As we visited various community professionals a vast sea of opportunity opened before our eyes. For example, a local counselor suggested that a divorce recovery group was desperately needed in the community and could be filled with referrals from his agency alone! An area funeral director recommended the establishment of a bereavement support group that would be available to widows and widowers who faced the crisis of grief without structured support. A government agency suggested the need for practical assistance ministry that would serve the frequently neglected and rapidly increasing senior-adult community. A hearing-impaired Christian told us that not a single local church was active in serving the more than one hundred deaf in our county. A conversation with a mental health professional revealed the shocking statistic that one out of every four adults is a victim of childhood sexual abuse, and the church has traditionally been silent about this physical and emotional exploitation of young lives.

Several hours of visits provided us with specific directions to many fields of service that were ripe for harvest. Never have these words of Christ in John 4:35 been more clearly illustrated to me than in our conversations with local community servants: "I tell you," Christ proclaimed to His disciples as He looked at the people in the community of Sychar, "Open your eyes and look at the fields! They are ripe for harvest." Indeed, in every community there are countless need groups that provide immediate opportunities for outreach. This is the first step in the development of any effective outreach or support group ministry: "Open your eyes and look at the fields."

Develop

When a particular need group is targeted, the development of a support group or outreach ministry generally requires six to nine months. The following elements are a part of the development process.

Inform Boards and Community Professionals

The leaders in the sponsoring church or Christian organization and the various community professionals who also serve the need group should be informed on a regular basis concerning the development and ongoing expansion of support group or outreach ministry. This foundational procedure is essential for their long-term support and for the expansion of the ministry.

Recruit and Select Leaders

According to Luke 10:2, recruiting and selecting leaders begins with prayer. God is the one who calls workers into ministry: "The harvest is plentiful but the workers are few. Ask the Lord of the harvest, therefore, to send out workers into his harvest field." In response to this challenge, our leaders gather often for prayer, boldly asking God to provide workers for specific ministries. These seasons of prayer are followed by an open discussion of possible candidates for leadership and then plans are made to contact those approved. As with the selection of small-group leaders, only those persons whose Christian lifestyle visibly reflects the biblical standards for leadership are considered. If the individuals approached, after a period of consideration, lack a clear calling and desire to launch the new ministry, we continue to wait, pray, and discuss. Some ministries required literally years of patience and prayer before God provided the appropriate leaders, yet in His own time He has *always* been faithful.

When seeking God's direction for potential support-group leaders, we commonly found called and willing hearts among those who have experienced and are constructively recovering from the particular kind of suffering that the support group has been designed to serve. Our support groups and outreach ministries are staffed primarily with lay volunteers. For example, the Bereavement Support Group staff consists of those who have themselves experienced the loss of a loved one. The majority of them lack formal training in grief counseling yet have graduated with honors from the school of suffering. They know well the emotions of grief as well as God's great adequacy in the midst of loss. The insights they share with other group attendees, Christian and non-Christian, are from their very hearts, faith, and lives. They are literally able to weep with those who weep.

Some support groups and outreach ministries include leaders who have a specific calling, burden, and gifts that enable them to effectively minister although they have not suffered in the same way as those whom they serve. For example, the staff that serves the visually impaired includes some members who have complete legal vision. This blend is needed to provide effective practical assistance in things like driving and reading.

Following the biblical precedent for leadership selection, we have found it advantageous for pastors or other competent leaders to hand-pick, after much prayer for spiritual guidance, the initial leadership core of four to six people who will staff the support group or outreach ministry. This careful, limited selection will ensure that the leaders display the

> *Some have not suffered in the same way as those they serve.*

necessary spiritual and emotional maturity to guide the support group or outreach ministry through the crucial infant stages. It is also beneficial to include, when possible, in the initial core group at least one devoutly Christian professional who is serving the targeted need group. The professional expertise, resources, referrals, and experience these people bring is quite beneficial.

The initial leadership core should make a commitment to meet at least twice a month over a twelve-month period with the goal of developing and launching a support group or outreach ministry. One founding member of the group should act as the chairperson and work with the pastoral staff or other assigned leadership.

Establish Purpose, Structure, Time Line

The basic areas that a core group will address during their initial months together will likely include defining the support group's purpose, developing the basic group structure, and establishing a tentative time line. A planning session form, appendix 2-A, provides a variety of questions to help leaders address and define these foundational areas. The types of questions used may vary depending on what type of support group or outreach ministry is being established.

It has been our experience that leaders require from four to six one-hour sessions before they have defined the assorted areas to the satisfaction of all present. The process of time is an essential ingredient in providing necessary "ownership" of the basic purpose and procedure and therefore it should not be rushed. As these areas are defined, the necessary information is provided for the development of promotional literature.

Next, a three-to-six-month time line is constructed from the planning session form. This time line should define the time and date of regular core-group meetings, the proposed date or month of the first support group/outreach ministry meeting, as well as a detailed account—events, promotion activities, specific times and dates—of what should be accomplished prior to the projected starting date, as in appendix 2-B.

> *Volunteers appreciate knowing specifically what tasks need to be accomplished.*

Create Ministry Guidelines

After a core group has invested several months formulating the plans for a ministry, their commitment to ensure that the group is launched and maintained often intensifies. Therefore, the presentation of ministry guidelines, appendix 2-C, to a core group at this stage is usually met with a high degree of receptivity. Correspondingly, volunteers appreciate knowing specifically what tasks need to be accomplished to develop and maintain the ministry. It has also been our experience that volunteers are more willing to participate if they have the opportunity to choose a field of service from among many options. The ministry guidelines provide the specific definition of task as well as a variety of ministry options.

Here, too, group ownership is vital. Our core-group leaders were given sample guidelines for evaluation and further development. Together we discussed which elements some felt were unnecessary and should be deleted; others suggested new areas they believed should be included among the responsibilities of the leaders. In some cases this procedure required several sessions. When the process was completed, they had a thorough list of what was required for launching and maintaining their group or ministry.

The next step is basic. The core-group members have to decide if they can facilitate the ministry tasks themselves or if they require additional volunteers to assist them. If they determine that their numbers are sufficient, they volunteer for the area(s) they would like to lead. The commitments of each core-group member are noted on the ministry guidelines sheets. If they feel that additional workers are needed, plans are made to secure them.

Expand the Core Group

A Sunday morning interview, appendix 2-D, with one of the core-group members, accompanied by appropriate promotional literature distributed in the bulletin, has proven to be an effective vehicle for securing additional volunteers. Those who indicate interest should be carefully interviewed by pastors and, if qualified, brought up to date as to the status of the group. In addition to those who respond to the Sunday morning promotion, names of prospective workers suggested by other core staff should be considered.

Following the period of recruitment, a core-group meeting is scheduled including the new members. The agenda for this meeting should include a get-acquainted time, an opportunity for update, questions and answers, and distribution of ministry guidelines for review, evaluation, and volunteer assignment. Although the ministry guidelines have been by this time fully revised by the original core group, it is important to allow incoming members the opportunity for input. Usually, however, the revisions are minimal. New members are afforded the opportunity to indicate the area(s) of service they would like to lead and these commitments are then recorded on the ministry guidelines sheets.

Launch

Clarify Core-Group Tasks

The core group should next focus in on the specific tasks outlined in the ministry guidelines that need to be completed prior to launching the first support group or outreach ministry meeting. As these tasks are discussed, the time line will also need to be updated. The date of the first support group or outreach ministry meeting should be determined at this point, along with the time, day, and place of regular core-group meetings.

Monthly meetings are, in my opinion, one of the most important elements in maintaining a disciplined and professional core group. The preprinted meeting agenda, appendix 2-E, is designed to establish mutual accountability among the members for the various organizational tasks they have agreed to fulfill. The agenda is also designed to ensure that the ministry maintains a personal emphasis.

When the support group is underway, the personal emphasis is maintained as the emotional, individual, and spiritual needs of support-group participants are considered by the core group on a monthly basis. For example, absentees are contacted along with first-time attendees. Support group members who seem particularly troubled are visited in their homes. The spiritual state of each is discussed in the confines of the core-group meeting with the goal of providing specific spiritual counsel or verbal witness. Although leaders who possess a gift of evangelism are usually the most willing to contact new group attendees whose commitment to Christ is unknown, every member of the core group is encouraged to seek opportunities to share "the hope that you have" (1 Pet. 3:15).

Promote

Promotion of the support group or outreach ministry should begin four to six weeks prior to the first meeting and should include every possible means and media available. In our small community of twenty thousand we utilize newspaper, radio, direct mail, and cable television. Page 114 is an illustration of an ad run in a local newspaper for the Bereavement Support Group. One of the core-group members can coordinate this facet of the ministry.

Promotional pamphlets are distributed widely to professional offices—doctors, optometrists, funeral directors, counselors, hospitals, and so on—and to every visitor to our church. We secured a space at the county fair to set up a table and distribute our materials to thousands who attend this annual event. Quarterly, a volunteer is in touch with the professional agencies who assist in the distribution of our materials to see if additional pamphlets are needed.

Establish Meeting Format

While our support groups and outreach ministries enjoy some variations in the style and format of their regular meetings, there are several elements that most have in common. The first and foremost of these components is the ministry of the Word. All of the groups and ministries are expected to provide the opportunity for their attendees to receive some type of biblical exhortation. In our support groups, for example, this is met through a short devotional message at the start of each meeting. The meditations are designed to link Bible passages and promises to the specific needs of group members.

Small groups allow people to test the waters.

Various outreach ministries have chosen various ways to accomplish this goal. For example, our ministry to the hearing impaired hosts a midweek Bible study attended by both Christians and non-Christians. Short-term missions volunteers enjoy devotions as a part of their regular team meetings. Our host families frequently invite their international friends to church services, while several are involved in evangelistic one-on-one Bible study. The youth outreach ministry provides a challenging devotional or evangelistic message during its regular activities and our practical assistance volunteers take time to pray, read Scripture, and share spiritual counsel with those whom they serve.

A second element common to many of our ministries, particularly our support groups, is the use of small groups. Most of our support groups begin their ninety-minute meetings with a welcome from the group facilitator who presents an overview of the topic for the evening. Next, group attendees introduce themselves and their guests. This preliminary portion of the meeting is followed by a short, biblical meditation and prayer. Then, a speaker, a film, or a staff member will present insights on the topic. The concluding segment of the meeting is spent discussing the topic in small groups of six to eight. One or two staff members facilitate each group.

In my opinion, the portion of the meeting spent in small-group exchange is second in importance only to the meditation. Most people are reluctant to share their intimate struggles with a large group, yet in a smaller group they are often more willing to reveal the pain they have been experiencing. Small groups allow people to test the waters to see if they will find genuine love, comfort, acceptance, and guidance. In these opportune moments the committed staff, through genuine listening and timely counsel, dispense redemptive biblical ministry. I have observed more emotional healing, spiritual reconciliation, and personal evangelism occurring in the small discussion groups than at any other point in the meeting!

Understand the Stages of Group Life

Within the core group. We have discovered that our core group moves through predictable stages of growth. Our core groups have notably experienced a courtship stage through the first six or so months of ministry formation. Generally the first support group or outreach ministry meetings are also well received. The enthusiasm at this stage is high as is the common commitment to other core-group members.

The bliss of courtship is frequently displaced by leadership conflicts or the kind of letdown one may feel after a vacation or after Christmas. Perhaps one staff member is not fulfilling his or her obligations or perhaps the support-group meetings do not seem to be growing as quickly as expected. The big push is over and the routine of ministry has settled in. The best way to assist staff members in working through this process is frank and open discussion. The attitude and commitment, therefore, of the pastors or other competent leaders to this process of dialogue is crucial.

The core-group meeting has proven to be the best place to deal with apparent conflict or emotional drain. A statement such as this has helped open the door for honest discussion: "I sense some frustration in the group at this point. Let's set aside our agenda for this meeting and talk about any difficulty we're experiencing." It may be advantageous to examine the stages of group life with the core group and ask them what they feel can be done to develop beyond this conflict stage.

Whatever method of evaluation is chosen, it is important that the process of interaction not be rushed. Without exception, all of our staff have moved beyond conflict to community when they have had opportunity to ventilate their frustrations and to suggest solutions. To ensure that openness and interpersonal growth continues, staff are led annually through an evaluation time during a regularly scheduled core-group meeting. They are asked to share their honest appraisal of the meetings and their personal involvement. They are also furnished with copies of the ministry guidelines and are provided the opportunity to commit themselves to continue in their present areas of service for the next year or to branch out into new fields. The annual evaluations have proven very beneficial as a forum for conflict resolution as well as for maintaining a current commitment to the tasks and ongoing life of the support group or outreach ministry.

Within the support group or outreach ministry. Each of our support groups and outreach ministries started with many of the exciting emotions of courtship but most never appeared to experience a noticeable conflict stage in their routine growth. The reasons for this, in my opinion, are two. First, a support group or outreach ministry tends to take on the attitude of its leaders. If the core group is in conflict, the support group will no doubt be affected by the tension. On the other hand, if the core group is in harmony, the support group will be influenced by the unity and community modeled by its leaders. The presence of faithful and caring staff provides a feeling of community that visitors experience as soon as they walk in the door and are warmly greeted. Without a doubt, a healthy core group is a foundational element in a healthy support group.

The second reason is perhaps linked to the changing attendance patterns that frequently occur in many of our support groups and outreach ministries. In the Bereavement Support Group, for example, one

> *If the core group is in conflict, the support group will be affected.*

individual who had been very consistent in her attendance suddenly started to miss meetings. When contacted about her absences by a caring and concerned staff member, she commented: "I have deeply appreciated the support that the group provided over the last several difficult months of my life, but I'm now feeling as though the backing and insights I've received have helped me see that I can indeed start to manage my own life. Don't worry, I'll be back—and I know where you are if I need you!" From time to time we would see this woman in our meetings and her growth was indeed evident. In our eyes, her withdrawal from the group was a victory, not an indication of loss or defeat. We celebrated the fact that God had used the group to encourage and strengthen her determination to manage her own life.

In corresponding fashion, we have observed that the support groups and outreach ministries that experience more regular attendance are likely to experience transitions through the various stages of group life. The Visually Impaired Support Association and the Deaf Fellowship, for example, fall into this category. Their members are in the process of coping rather than of recovery. Therefore they find strength in meeting frequently with others who are also in the process of coping. With groups such as these we have found it advantageous to spend an entire meeting encouraging group members to ventilate any frustrations and to offer program suggestions. This meeting can be undertaken at a time when group conflict is evident or on a regular basis to help maintain community.

Plan for the Summer

The core group should allow the support group or outreach ministry members to help determine the need to meet through the summer months. Our Deaf Fellowship overwhelmingly declared that their summer months were too filled with other activities that would conflict with regular meetings. For them, a nine-month program was best. The visually impaired, on the other hand, were equally vocal about maintaining regular meetings through the summer months. They suggested, however, that the format change to include picnics and other social outings. The other support groups and outreach ministries enjoyed a similar flexibility in establishing their summer agendas.

Chapter Six

RENEWAL THROUGH THE ADULT SUNDAY SCHOOL

In many evangelical churches the adult Sunday school provides a natural context for the implementation of the principles and patterns of renewal. Classes usually enjoy an established base of strong leadership, consistent Bible teaching, and a core of committed regular attendees—three important factors in church renewal. In addition, the closest friendships many Christians experience in the church are found among other class participants, friendships that spill over into the life of the class and that provide natural opportunities for a lifestyle and a proclamational witness to non-Christians who may attend.

Why, if these things are true, do we often fail to experience significant inward and outward growth in a majority of our adult Sunday school classes? Is the problem a lack of willingness or commitment? Not necessarily. In my experience, most people want to experience significant inward and outward growth through their Sunday school classes. I believe the problems fall into two broad categories: *intentionality* and *strategy*. The classes lack specific, intentional strategies to promote fellowship, outreach, and assimilation. My home church designed a Sunday school growth task force to address this problem.

Develop

Inform Boards and Adult-Class Teachers

The leaders in a local church or Christian organization must be fully informed and must give comprehensive approval prior to the implementation of a Sunday school growth task force. The board that oversees the Christian education ministry, in particular, should have the opportunity to dialogue on these concepts and to affirm the implementation of the diagnostic process. The endorsement of the governing boards often provides additional significance to a Christian education project in the eyes of many teachers and students.

After the affirmation of the governing boards has been secured, each adult-class teacher should also have the opportunity to examine the task force's philosophy, design, and materials. Teachers may suggest additions or alterations in the forms. They should also be asked to recommend two individuals from the class they teach as representative members of the task force. The participation of the teachers in the task force is welcomed and encouraged, but not essential. What must be gained in this initial stage is the teachers' affirmation of the task force and their willingness to support its insights and recommendations.

Select Leaders

Thus, each adult class will be represented on the task force by two class members. Individuals who demonstrate a model Christian life and enjoy the respect of other class attendees should also be prayerfully sought to serve on the task force. Teachers, class presidents, officers, and the like are natural candidates. Appointments should be made with each candidate, at which time the task force's philosophy, design, and materials can be considered. Those who are willing to be a part of the process form the task-force team for their class. They will attend four one-hour task-force meetings and will fulfill the assignments noted on the worksheets, appendixes 3-B to 3-E.

Evolve Strategies

All leaders who commit themselves to participate in the task force receive a letter, appendix 3-A, that contains the basic agenda, dates, definitions of terms, and outline for the four meetings. Also in the letter is the preparation worksheet, appendix 3-B, for session one. This worksheet, as well as the others used in sessions two, three, and four, appendix 3-C to 3-E, maintain an intentional loyalty to the Biblical Principles of Renewal. For example, group and individual prayer and a brief biblical exhortation take place at each task force meeting. Also, each team is encouraged to develop various fellowship, outreach, and assimilation strategies to accommodate the unique needs and expectations of the people in its class. Mutual accountability is a deliberate part of each session and team members are challenged, through the development of outreach strategies, to be involved in intentional evangelism.

Session 1: What worked before? The focus of the first session is to gain insights as to the effective styles of fellowship, outreach, and assimilation that have been a part of the history of each particular class. Preparation Worksheet 1, appendix 3-B, which is intended to be completed prior to this session, affords task-force members this opportunity. An understanding of the history of each class provides helpful background information when selecting or designing fellowship, outreach, and assimilation strategies that are distinctive for each.

Session 2: What works now? Session 2 begins by furnishing task force members the occasion to share the methods of fellowship, outreach, and assimilation that are now proving effective in their classes. These ideas are recorded by each participant. Next, each task force team contacts four additional members of their class to obtain their opinions as to the effectiveness of the various fellowship, outreach, and assimilation methods that have been and are being used. The team compiles all the information developed to this point and narrows it down to recommend one strategy in each area: fellowship, outreach, and assimilation. Preparation Worksheet 2, appendix 3-C, assists task force members in accomplishing these assignments.

Session 3: What will work from now on? Task force participants begin this third meeting by reporting their tentative fellowship, outreach, and assimilation strategies. Then, Preparation Worksheet 3, appendix 3-D, is distributed. The assignments on this worksheet help the team finalize strategies and expand them to include a nine-month time line for implementation. Ministry guidelines for the position of hospitality coordinator, appendix 3-E, are also provided during this session. These guidelines will assist task force members with recruiting the leaders to coordinate the recommended strategies. Prospective candidates for the positions of the hospitality coordinators and assistants are next suggested from among the class members and recorded. It has been our experience that task force members often recommend themselves! Finally, the strategies, related events, and candidates' names are reported to the class teacher, president, and two other class members. Each of these persons is asked for input, evaluation, revision (if necessary), and recommendation.

Session 4: Implementation. At the start of this meeting, task-force participants report on their progress to date. After the reports are given, Preparation Worksheet 4 (appendix 3-F) and the materials for the hospitality coordinators (appendix 3-G) are distributed and reviewed. Special emphasis is placed on securing the hospitality coordinators and their committees of assistants. A specific time is also established in cooperation with each teacher, to present the proposed nine-month time line of events, as well as the vision for growth, to the Sunday school class. Next, a meeting date and time is agreed upon for the one-month evaluation, at which time the various strategies developed by each team are expected to be in progress. Session four concludes with a period of overall evaluation.

Launch Visitation Teams

Visiting and assimilating new attendees is directed by the hospitality coordinator but often is shared among members of the hospitality committee and the Sunday school class. Class members who possess a gift of evangelism are strong additions

> *Class members who possess a gift of evangelism are strong additions to visitation teams.*

to the visitation team particularly when contacts with unchurched individuals or families are requested. The implementation of the visiting process is quite simple. As pastors make routine calls on new church attendees, they develop a sense as to which adult class the new attendees might feel most comfortable with. A visitation form, appendix 3-G, containing some basic information about the family or individual visited, along with a response postcard, is sent to the hospitality coordinator in the class.

Completed visits are reported to pastors through response postcards, which often furnish valuable insights gleaned from the visit as well as provide a form of accountability. If the postcard is not received within three weeks, the individual assigned to visit is contacted. A master file of all contacts accomplished is maintained for future reference.

Evaluate

Meetings for evaluation at one month and at six months build ongoing accountability into the process of Sunday school renewal. A meeting is held one month after session four, at which time each task force team discusses the information on Preparation Worksheet 4, appendix 3-F. Each report will include the name of the hospitality coordinator and committee members and the response of the class to the presentation of the proposed strategies and time line. This information from each team is then duplicated and filed.

Six months later, task-force members again meet to report their progress. Previously established time lines are retrieved from the file and compared with the progress report of each task force team. Those who have fallen behind are encouraged to renew their commitment to pursue the goals they had established and the events they had planned. Correspondingly, the classes who are maintaining their agendas provide a valuable model to the others who have not made as much progress.

The task-force team is called together on an annual basis to establish strategies for the upcoming year. Preparation Worksheet 5, to be used along with a new Preparation Worksheet 4, was designed to facilitate this process. In the first of two sessions, a class's task-force members, teacher, hospitality coordinator, and hospitality committee members meet to discuss and evaluate the fellowship, outreach, and assimilation strategies from the year just completed. The names of additional or replacement people for this leadership team are discussed and plans are made to contact them. In the second meeting, the group, including any new members, decides which strategies require revision and which have been effective. Dialogue is continued until the group reaches a consensus concerning the fellowship, outreach, and assimilation strategies for the coming year. The agreed-upon strategies are reported to the class. The group meets again in one month and in six months for follow-up evaluations.

RELATED MATERIALS FOR RENEWAL THROUGH SMALL GROUPS

1-A: Biblical Principles of Renewal

Principles of Evangelism

1. Evangelism and renewal are, at their foundations, sovereign works of the triune God. The church's response is to maintain an attitude of dependency in prayer and in works of obedient service.
2. The New Testament church used a variety of evangelistic activities and methods. Most were chosen to meet the specific physical, spiritual, or emotional needs of the individuals or groups it was attempting to reach. Evangelism was people-centered rather than program-centered.
3. There is a New Testament gift of evangelism.
4. Lifestyle evangelism is basic to proclamational evangelism.
5. Every member of the body of Christ is expected to evangelize.
6. Leaders are exhorted to model evangelism and a consistent Christian lifestyle.

Principles of Discipleship

1. Members of the body of Christ are dependent on, and accountable to, one another.
2. Small groups are often used by the Holy Spirit to initiate and to sustain discipleship in the body.
3. The ministry of the Word is essential to the growth of the body.

✳   ✳   ✳

1-B: Share-Group Covenant

Group name _____ Date _____

Goals for the period *[usually three months]* from _____ to _____.

Keep the following insights in mind as you use this sheet to develop specific goals and plans for group and individual growth.

Are your goals and plans *ownable?* That is, can you individually and as a group fully embrace them as your own?

Are your goals and plans *measurable?* That is, are they specific and well defined enough so that you will be able at a future point to say, "Yes, [we, I] accomplished this," or, "No, [we, I] did not accomplish this."

Are your goals and plans *stretching?* That is, do they stretch you and the group a bit beyond the time, resources, desires, and abilities you now believe you have, so that you are pressed toward growth in dependence on God for His help in fulfilling them?

Group Purpose (fill in blanks)

The purpose of our group is to grow

in our love for, and commitment to, Christ by

in our love for, and commitment to, each other by

in our love for, and commitment to, our neighbor by

Group Meetings

1. Meeting place(s)

2. Day of the week and frequency of meeting

3. Meetings will begin at _____ and end at _____

4. We will keep the following schedule in each meeting

5. Refreshments, if desired, will be the responsibility of

6. Name(s) of the group leader(s)

7. Attendance commitment to the share group meetings

Inward Growth Goals

Group and personal Bible study, prayer, and other spiritual growth goals

Specific plans to fulfill these goals

Outward Growth Goals

>   Record the names of two or more friends and neighbors we desire to include in our group.
>
>   Specific plans to serve and contact these people
>
>   Name(s) of one or two individuals who will represent our group at the monthly leaders' meeting

✳   ✳   ✳

1-C: Share-Group Introductory Studies

Session 1

Fellowship (30 minutes)

A major goal of the first session is for group members to get acquainted with each other. Using one question at a time, encourage each person to answer. After all have answered, go on to the next question until you have finished them all.

>   A. Please tell us your name, where you lived between the ages of seven and twelve, and how many brothers and sisters were living at home at that time.
>   B. How did you heat your house?
>   C. Who was the "warmest" person in your life?
>   D. When did God become more than a word to you?

Explore (20 minutes)

A. Distribute and give an overview of the share-group covenant sheets. Be sure to highlight the following:
   1. Review the instructions and group purpose. Mention that each group will develop its own agenda, inward and outward growth goals, and specific plans to fulfill each goal. This process may require several weeks.
   2. One group member (or at the most, two) will represent your group at the monthly leaders' meeting. A guideline sheet describing that task is attached to this material [appendix 1 -D].
   3. The goals are usually developed for a three-month time span; groups will then evaluate their progress and establish new goals.

   Note: Groups are encouraged not to attempt to develop goals until next session so that ample time can be given to the goal-setting process.

B. Discuss and together develop the group agenda. Be careful to allow all opinions to be expressed and a consensus of opinion to be reached on each item. Have group members record decisions on their share-group covenant.
C. Ask each group member to come to the next meeting prepared with suggestions for inward and outward growth goals as well as specific plans to fulfill each suggested goal.

Close (10 minutes)

Break into pairs and share a specific need each expects to encounter this week. Pray with each other regarding these needs.

Session 2

Fellowship (20 minutes)

A. Request that group members each find one other individual that he or she doesn't know at all or doesn't know well. After members are paired off, they should exchange their names and tell three significant things about themselves (vocation, hobbies, favorite foods, and the like). Individuals should then introduce their partners to the entire group—including the various new things they learned about them.
B. Individually read Acts 1:1–14 and note one or two verses that especially speak to you. After you finish, share with your partner the verses you chose and why they seem especially significant to you.

Explore the Passage (as much time as needed)

Commentary/Facilitator Notes

Verses 4–5. Note the centrality of the Holy Spirit in all aspects of ministry. Ministry without the energy and power of the Holy Spirit is dead, man-made ministry that will have little effect for the kingdom. This passage is a parallel to the words of Christ in Luke 24:49.

Verse 6. The disciples still thought Jesus was going to set up an earthly kingdom.

Verse 7. Jesus tells them that their business is not to worry about when that kingdom will come, but to be busy at the tasks of the kingdom.

Verse 8. "Power" in the Greek is *dunamis.* We get our English word *dynamite* from this root. The writer is illustrating the explosive potential of the Holy Spirit in the lives of believers who are yielded to His control. "Witness" in the Greek is *martur.* This word means one who is totally yielded. We get our English word *martyr* from this root. *Witness* in the New Testament is much more than evangelism. It involves a total lifestyle—actions, attitudes, motives, and words.

"When the Holy Spirit comes on you." Note again the centrality of the Holy Spirit in ministry. We work with Him. He is really the one who changes hearts and draws people to Christ through us (John 16:7–10).

"in Jerusalem, and in all Judea and Samaria, and to the ends of the earth." Note how Jesus challenged them to an impossible task—impossible without divine help and intervention. We must also be sure the goals we establish are beyond our human ability and press us to the Source of power and help.

Verse 14. "Constantly in prayer." The disciples were burdened with an impossible task so they were pressed to pray. We too become a praying people when our tasks and goals are beyond our own ability to perform. Prayer is mentioned at least twenty-four times in Acts!

Explore Further

Supply everyone with pens, paper, and a share-group covenant, and divide into small groups of two to four.

A. Encourage the members of the small group to express their personal expectations and recommendations for the inward and outward growth goals as well as specific plans to fulfill the goals. One member of each group should list the recommendations and be prepared to report them to the whole group.

B. After each group has had adequate time to discuss, ask a representative from each to report its recommendations to the entire group. The various suggestions should be listed on a piece of newsprint or poster board so they can be seen by everyone.

C. In an open discussion format, examine the goals and corresponding plans. Prayerfully decide which you should pursue as a group. As the goals are discussed, remember to make them ownable, measurable, and stretching.

> *Important: Goals should not be adopted until consensus has been reached by the entire group. This may take an extra session.*

Close

Be sure to close each session with prayer for group and individual needs. Prayer should also be offered for those individuals the group is planning to contact and invite.

✻   ✻   ✻

1-D: Ministry Guidelines—Share-Group Leader

Purpose

A share-group leader provides biblical, accountable, and caring leadership for his or her share group.

Personnel

One or two leaders will represent each share group. New share-group leaders will be selected and/or approved by the consensus of the share-group leaders as the need arises. Their selection should be based on spiritual gifts, maturity, and a Christian lifestyle that visibly reflects the biblical standards for leadership.

Procedure

Share-group leaders will
- strongly affirm the group purpose as well as the inward and outward growth goals outlined in the share-group covenant;
- facilitate the group's goal-setting sessions and lead in the fulfillment of its inward and outward growth goals;
- maintain careful attendance records and contact absentees within a few days following their absence from the share group;
- attend monthly leaders' meetings (if your group has two leaders, only one need attend) and present attendance records along with a general progress report;
- serve for twelve months, from September to September, after which a renewed commitment to lead can be established if desired.

Provisions

Reasonable and necessary study materials and supplies can be secured through the church's established procedure.

* * *

1-E: Annual Flow Chart
for Share-Group Ministry

March

Evaluate the Annual Flow Chart for Share-Group
Ministry and suggest changes as needed.

April

Review the form, Two Types of Group Personalities.
Discuss the uses of this tool to help share-group
members identify their particular strengths and
differences.

Distribute, review, and evaluate the Strategies for a
Growing Family form. Suggest changes as needed.
Discuss and suggest the potential use of these forms
in helping groups develop their outreach
applications.

Each leader should discuss with his or her share group,
prior to the May meeting, its proposed summer agenda.

May

Review the agenda each group has established for the
summer.

Discuss and evaluate any responses to the Two Types
of Group Personalities and Strategies for a Growing Family forms. Suggest changes as needed.

Introduce and evaluate plans for the fall promotion.

June/July

Recruit leaders for additional groups. Hold an orienta-
tion seminar for new leaders.

August

Finalize and initiate fall promotional plans including:
  Sunday morning interview with bulletin insert;
  promotion in each adult Sunday school class;
  promotion in the church newsletter;
  individual invitations from each share group (this
    will mean that each share group develops a list
    of people to invite).
Established groups set a regular meeting day and time
  (if meetings have been infrequent over the summer).
  Begin regular meetings by early September.
The Strategies for a Growing Family and the Two
  Types of Group Personalities forms will be distributed and reviewed. Each share group will examine the Strategies for a Growing Family form and
  come to a consensus as to which option(s) will best
  fit their group. This exercise should be completed
  prior to the September leaders' meeting. Pastors
  are available to meet with any group during this
  evaluation time.

September

Evaluate fall promotional efforts:
  Sunday morning interview with bulletin insert;
  promotion in each adult Sunday school class;
  promotion in the church newsletter;
  individual invitations from each share group.
Group leaders report decisions concerning
  groups' plans for meeting and study;
  groups' plans for assimilating new members;
  leaders' commitments to serve for another year.
Decisions are made as to placement of new registrants.
  New groups are expected to start by mid-October.

New members being invited into established groups should also be contacted by that time.

Books, study guides, and other materials appropriate for small-group study will be supplied through the church's established procedure.

Share-group covenants and introductory studies will be distributed and reviewed. Leaders will present their groups' completed covenants at the next meeting.

October

Each leader will report the agenda and inward and outward growth goals his or her group has established for the fall.

The information concerning stages of group life will be discussed [the material in appendix 1-J may be useful to facilitate discussion].

November

The Biblical Principles of Renewal [appendix 1-A] will be reviewed and discussed.

December

Distribute and study information that will meet current specific needs of group leaders and group participants.

January

Distribute group evaluations, to be completed by each share group prior to the February leaders' meeting.

Complete and discuss leaders' evaluations. Recommend, as necessary, any changes

February

Discuss completed group evaluations. Recommend, as necessary, any changes.

1-F: Share-Group Promotional Materials

Promotional Interview

Dear_____,

Thank you for agreeing to be interviewed this coming Sunday morning as a part of our share-group promotion. We will conduct the interview during the announcement period of both services. It should require no more than five minutes.

I will ask you to respond to the following:

1. Describe a typical share-group meeting.
2. Some people are afraid they will be put on the spot to pray aloud or to speak in front of a group. Has that been a difficulty in your group?
3. How have you grown personally and spiritually as a result of your share group?
4. Is there anything else that you would like to tell us about your experience?

I look forward to spending this time with you. If you have any questions, please feel free to contact me.

Sunday School Class Promotional

Teacher's Letter and Agenda

Dear_____,

Thank you for your teaching ministry! We value your contribution in this way. I want to update you as to some plans suggested by our share-group ministry that will affect your class this fall. We would like your permission to take ten minutes at the start of class time on Sunday September _____ for a representative from our share-group ministry, who is also a member of your class, to tell briefly about his or her experience in share groups, to field questions, and to give an opportunity for class response. We have found that our groups have grown through peer contacts and thus Sunday school formats such as this one are very helpful.

Please let me know if you have any difficulty with this request. If I *don't* hear from you, I'll give our ministry volunteers the go ahead.

Worker's Letter and Agenda

Dear_____,

At our last share-group leaders' meeting we established September _____ as the Sunday morning to promote share groups in each adult Sunday school class. To accomplish this, we planned the following low-key approach: The first ten minutes at the beginning of class (your teacher has already been notified) will be set aside to allow those from your class who have previously been involved in share groups to

1. tell a bit about their experiences in share groups (what the format is like, how they have grown personally through the experience, and so forth);
2. field any questions the class might have;
3. circulate the attached registration form for class members to indicate interest.

Will you address your Sunday school class in this way? Other class members also involved in share groups can feel free to add to your comments. Please let me know if you have any questions or difficulty with this request. The completed registration sheets can be left in my office. Thanks for your help! If I *don't* hear from you, I will send you a reminder note prior to September _____.

Share-Group Registration Form

Adults of all ages enjoyed participating in share groups last year. If you are not yet involved, here is your opportunity to join them!

What Is a Share Group?
A share group consists of about eight to twelve people who gather to grow personally and spiritually.

How Long Do They Last?
The share groups usually meet for about three months at a time, after which the group decides if it wants to continue. A typical meeting will last about sixty to ninety minutes.

When and Where Do They Meet?
Most groups meet in the homes of group members who express a desire to host. The specific time, place, and day is decided upon by each group.

What Are the Meetings Like?

Each share group develops its own agenda and goals. Following the initial planning session, a typical meeting usually includes fellowship, learning through Bible study, sharing, and prayer.

Would You Like to Be Involved?

Indicate your interest and someone will contact you with further information. Feel free to attend one or two meetings just to see what they are like without feeling obligated to commit yourself to the entire three months.

Name/Phone	Day(s) or Evening(s) Available
1.	
2.	
3.	
4.	
5.	
6.	

❋   ❋   ❋

WHEN YOU DESIRE TO BE A PART OF A SMALL, CARING FELLOWSHIP OF BELIEVERS . . .

THERE ARE PEOPLE WHO CARE. . . .

A SHARE GROUP FAMILY

SHARE GROUPS

Adults of all ages have enjoyed participating in share groups! If you're not already involved, we want to provide you the opportunity to join!

WHAT ARE THEY?

A share group consists of about 8–12 adults who gather weekly to grow together personally and spiritually. Each group develops its own outreach goals.

HOW LONG DO THEY LAST?

The share groups usually meet for about three months at a time, after which they evaluate and decide if it wants to continue. A typical weekly meeting will last for one to two hours.

WHEN AND WHERE DO WE MEET?

Most groups meet in homes of group members who express a desire to host. The specific time, place, and day of the week is decided upon by each group.

WHAT ARE MEETINGS LIKE?

Each share group develops its own agenda and goals. Following this initial planning session, a typical meeting usually begins with fellowship and contains a time of learning, sharing, and prayer. No one is put on the spot to share or pray aloud. New participants are welcome at any meeting!

HOW CAN I BECOME INVOLVED?

Indicate below your interest and you will be contacted with further information. You are welcome to attend one or two meetings just to see what they are like without feeling obligated to commit yourself for the entire three months.

Yes, I am interested in learning more about a share group.

Please contact me with information about a:
(check one)

_____ mixed age group   _____ 40s–50s group
_____ college group   _____ 60+ group
_____ seminary group   _____ Other (please describe)
_____ 18–25 group
_____ 20s–30s group

Name _____ Phone _____

Evenings or days available: (circle)

M   T   W   TH   F   S

1-G: Ministry Guidelines—Share-Group Captain

Purpose

The share-group captain supervises a cluster of two other share-group leaders.

Personnel

The share-group captain will be chosen from among the share-group leaders.

Procedure

Share-group captains will
- actively affirm all the areas of procedure listed in the ministry guidelines for share-group leaders;
- meet with a cluster of two other group leaders during the monthly leaders' meeting to
  1. consider the overall progress of each group
  2. hear the concerns of the group leaders about themselves and about group members
  3. offer appropriate biblical suggestions and counsel
  4. record attendance figures for each share group in a master book
  5. encourage contacts with any group member who has missed two or more consecutive meetings
  6. lead the cluster in prayer for every participant in their three share groups
- meet with the pastoral staff, as needed, to discuss concerns about any of his or her supervised groups;
- continue contact with group leaders as deemed necessary throughout the month.

* * *

1-H: Share-Group Attendance Registration

Group Name _____

Attendance for the Month of _____

	Weeks				
Group Members	1	2	3	4	5

1. _____
2. _____
3. _____
4. _____
5. _____
6. _____
7. _____
8. _____
9. _____
10. _____
11. _____
12. _____
13. _____
14. _____
15. _____

Attendance Information: (P)resent (A)bsent (V)isitor

Note: Leader, please contact those who were absent last week as well as visitors. Your absentee contacts will help you identify any needs they might have. Also, update them as to the location of the next meeting. Your visitor contacts help them feel a part of the group and allow you to field any questions and to invite them back to the next group session.

* * *

1-I: Master Attendance Registration

Group Name ______________________________

Attendance for the Month of ____________________

Group Members	Weeks 1	2	3	4	5
1. ________					
2. ________					
3. ________					
4. ________					
5. ________					
6. ________					
7. ________					
8. ________					
9. ________					
10. ________					
11. ________					
12. ________					

Attendance Information: (P)resent (A)bsent (V)isitor

* * *

1-J: Stages of Group Life

The following questions are designed to guide your group's discussion of the stages of group life.

List the three stages of group life (review pp. 44–47).

1.
2.
3.

Which stage do you feel your group is experiencing? Should your group mature from this stage to the next one? If yes, discuss how this might be done. What struggles do you believe your group will encounter along the way? *Note thoughts or comments from the discussion that you consider important.*

Enjoy the cartoon visualizing various types of personalities of group members. Starting with number one, label each character with a descriptive name.

* * *

1-K: Share-Group Evaluation

Please complete each statement as directed. Feel free to add any comments.

1. Over the past several months (circle one)
    My ability to share openly and honestly with others in my group has
    improved   **remained the same**   **declined**

    My personal spiritual disciplines (prayer, Bible study) have
    improved   **remained the same**   **declined**

    My personal attitude toward outreach has
    improved   **remained the same**   **declined**

    My personal practice of outreach has
    improved   **remained the same**   **declined**

2. If you answered "improved" for any of the statements, please tell what factors caused the improvement(s).

3. What can I do to increase my outreach? What can the group do to help me accomplish this?

4. What can I do to grow in my relationships?

5. Additional comments:

Name (optional) _____ Date _____

* * *

1-L: Share-Group Leaders' Evaluation

Please complete each statement as directed.

1. I have found the most valuable part of the share group leaders' meetings to be (circle one)

    prayer/   **informal**   **training/**
    Bible study   **sharing**   **materials**

    Other (please describe)

2. For me, the most frustrating part of the share-group leaders' meetings is

3. I would like to see these area(s) of training in future leaders' meetings

4. Other comments concerning the group sessions, materials, experiences, or training

Name (optional) _____ Date _____

* * *

1-M: Two Types of Group Personalities

The Pioneer

The pioneer is the group risk taker. Pioneers like new ideas and are threatened by either risks or new ideas. They may be heard saying: "This idea has some possibilities—let's try it!" Pioneers are generally self-starters and enjoy the challenge of share groups that are just beginning and that need foundational leadership. They are often goal- and process-oriented people. Pioneers may find themselves losing interest in areas of ministry that have moved into a basic routine. There are usually several pioneers in every group.

The Rancher

A rancher likes to keep the home fires burning. Ranchers enjoy stability and may express reservations when confronted by change. They may be heard saying: "This is working so well—why change it?" Ranchers are often people-oriented and will take special care to ensure that group members are cared for. They are most at home when their group falls into a comfortable and predictable pattern and basic routine. A change is more readily accepted by a rancher when understood as benefiting people rather than as just expanding the program.

Group Observations

Take a moment to categorize the people in your group as either pioneers or ranchers. Remember this is not a critical evaluation because neither is superior to the other;

both are necessary for a strong group. In fact, our differences are by God's design and therefore should be seen as strengths. After this individual exercise is completed, the entire group can express one at a time to each member the gifts he or she brings to the group as either a pioneer or rancher.

Name   **Category**

                                            (P=pioneer R=rancher)

1. _____   _____
2. _____   _____
3. _____   _____
4. _____   _____
5. _____   _____
6. _____   _____
7. _____   _____
8. _____   _____

* * *

1-N: Strategies for a Growing Family

Our share group will soon experience growing pains! The biblical priority of outreach we've established, coupled with the desire to encourage others to be a part of the expanding circle of share-group families, will be expressed through a major promotion in September. That's exciting—and uncomfortable—news; exciting, because others will soon experience the fellowship, love, and discipleship that we have enjoyed; uncomfortable, because established groups will incorporate new attendees, and new leaders will emerge to facilitate new groups.

Several ideas are suggested here to assist your group to assimilate new members. You are free to suggest your own option as well. Your group will not need to make a final decision until after the fall promotion when the specific number of people who are interested in becoming involved in share groups is known. May God guide you as you lend your hearts and lives to help establish plans for incorporating the new sheep He desires to bring into our share group.

Option 1: Your group decides, based on the need, to send out a "missionary" team who will lead a new group. After the new group has been established and new leaders have emerged (usually about six months), the missionary team has the option to return to their original group if they so desire. The original group supports their missionaries with prayer and encouragement.

Option 2: Your group decides, based upon the need, to divide in half with each group assimilating several new members. The two groups may continue to meet together monthly or quarterly for fellowship so that ties established in the original group can be maintained.

Option 3: Your group decides to remain together and, based upon the need, to include three to four new share group registrants into your family.

Option 4: Your group decides on the following strategy to help assimilate our growing family.

RELATED MATERIALS FOR RENEWAL THROUGH SUPPORT GROUPS AND OUTREACH MINISTRIES

2-A: Core-Group Planning Session

1. Please tell us your name, your vocation, and your particular interest in helping to develop this group.

2. Brainstorm on the following three areas of group development.
   Core-group meetings. How often should we meet? How long will our meetings last? Time and date of our regular meeting?

   Purpose. What will be the fundamental purpose of our support group? Does this purpose reflect consideration of spiritual, emotional, social, and educational needs? Can the purpose be recorded in one sentence?

   Procedure. What should the monthly support group meetings be like (time limits, location, spiritual emphasis, basic agenda, and so forth)? When will we be ready to start? What needs to be accomplished prior to starting? How should we get the word into the community? Begin to develop a time line for these things to occur.

2-B: Time Line

This is a sample time line adapted from that of the core group of the Bereavement Support Group of Park Street Brethren Church.

Sunday, July 19. Interview our director before the congregation to enlighten the church about our ministry and to enlist additional volunteers to serve in the core group. Our completed promotional pamphlet will be included in the bulletin that day.

Thursday, July 23. Next meeting of total core group. The purpose of this meeting is to report the names of those who volunteered as a result of the Sunday morning interview and the names of other individuals whom we believe would also be an asset to our leadership core group. Between July 23 and 30 staff members will contact these prospective workers by phone or home visit to give an overview of our group purpose, philosophy, history, and future plans. Invite those interested in serving with us to our July 30 meeting.

Thursday, July 30. Welcome new volunteers and provide a get-acquainted time. Distribute and go over ministry guidelines. Members will evaluate, suggest changes, and indicate where they see themselves fitting in.

Thursday, July 30 through Monday, August 10. Meet with our individual ministries to develop our tasks.

Monday, August 10. Whole group meets to report on progress and to evaluate, suggest changes to, and chart future core-group dates and direction. Set date for the first support group meeting.

September. Start community promotion. Specific plans for promotion will be established and delegated at this meeting. Schedule at least one dress-rehearsal support group with core members prior to October.

October. Launch the support group sometime this month.

2-C: Ministry Guidelines—Bereavement Support Group

Ministry assistants

	Name	Phone
1.		
2.		
3.		
4.		
5.		
6.		
7.		

Each of the following tasks needs to be completed for each support group meeting. Each task or group of tasks will be the responsibility of one or more ministry assistants. The initials of the person(s) responsible can be placed in the blank before to each item.

Setup

_____ Arrange physical setup of meeting place.
_____ Prepare refreshment table (table, hot water, coffee, cups, and so forth).

_____ Set up book table; keep current with one or two new selections at each meeting; have free materials and books to loan; be available before and after meetings to answer questions.

_____ Put up signs to direct people to the meeting place.

_____ Perform other tasks deemed necessary for setup (please list).

Meeting Agenda

_____ Host support-group meetings.

 1. Extend a warm welcome to those attending for the first time as well as to old friends. Ask everyone to give his or her name. Be sure new people are introduced and their names recorded.

 2. Explain the format of the meeting; announce the topic for the evening; emphasize confidentiality; answer questions; tell location of book table, restrooms, refreshment table; and specify ending time.

 3. Pray for requests of those present.

_____ Provide appropriate biblical devotional thought of five to ten minutes.

_____ Plan a twelve-month agenda of support group meetings that includes a wide range of topics, speakers, and films. Contact speakers and arrange for films well in advance. Be responsible for all the details of speakers' transportation and financial remuneration.

_____ Perform other tasks deemed necessary for each meeting (please list).

Publicity

_____ Coordinate all publicity—radio, newspaper,

television, and other means developed in core-group meetings.

_____ Once a quarter (December, March, June, September) visit the social agencies and other places where pamphlets have been distributed to check their supply and remind them of our services. Continue to look for new places to distribute material.

_____ Coordinate the mailings of reminder cards with updated information on the next meeting one week in advance of the meeting.

_____ Perform other tasks deemed necessary for publicity (please list).

Follow-Up

_____ Greet each member and visitor at the support group meeting.

_____ Circulate the visitor registration sheet at each meeting. Keep an attendance list and send a copy to the pastor within a week of the meeting.

_____ Send visitors a personal welcome card within a week of their visit.

_____ Contact, via note or phone call, any regular attendees who were absent from the meeting.

_____ Coordinate home visits to new attendees (usually after their second visit).

_____ Coordinate practical assistance to regular and prospective attendees.

_____ Coordinate social events for holidays.

_____ Perform other tasks deemed necessary for follow-up (please list).

* * *

2-D: Support Group Promotional Interview

This interview is to be conducted during the church's morning worship service(s) with one of the support group staff members.

1. Please describe the purpose of the Bereavement Support Group.
2. What is the need in our community for a group such as this?
3. The core group is preparing for the first meeting. The ministry is expanding and there is opportunity for additional people to join. Describe some of the areas of service the staff will perform and how someone in the congregation can become involved.
4. Is there anything else you would like to tell us?

✱ ✱ ✱

2-E: Core-Group Meeting Agenda

For the Month of _____ Year _____

1. Support Group Evaluation

Evaluate the previous support group meeting. Note what was done well and what needs improvement. How can we do it better?

directing signs

introductory comments, welcome

devotions, prayer

speaker or other presentation

discussion

room arrangement, refreshments

fellowship time

book table

other

2. *Group Contacts*

A.   Report on contacts completed or assistance provided to group members within the last month. Note type of assistance given.

B.   Would another contact be helpful? If yes, list below names of individuals and volunteers who agree to contact or assist others in making contacts.

C.   Report the names of visitors. Were welcome cards sent to each?

D.   Review attendance information. Are there other group members who would benefit from a phone call, spiritual guidance, a card, a home visit, or some type of practical assistance? Are there some who may not know Christ? List names of individuals and volunteers who agree to contact or assist them.

3. *Plans*

A.   Present plans for the next support group meeting. Are all the details secured? If not, what needs to be done and who will be responsible to see that it is finished?

B.   Would the group benefit from a social event? If so, note below dates, plans, and person(s) responsible for coordination.

C.   Review the twelve-month calendar of future meeting topics, speakers, and so forth. Do changes need to be made? If yes, which staff member(s) will update this information at the next core-group meeting?

4. Publicity

A.   Evaluate the publicity (radio, newspaper, cable TV, monthly reminder mailer, and so on). Note suggestions or needs.

B.   Is it time to again visit social agencies or other places where our pamphlets have been distributed to check on their supply and remind them of our services? At what other new places can we distribute our material? List volunteers and suggestions.

C.   What other ways can you suggest to promote our support group?

5. Other Business

6. Group Prayer

Note: Please provide the pastor with a copy of this report within a week following the staff meeting.

WHEN DEATH HAS
TOUCHED YOUR LIFE . . . .

THERE ARE PEOPLE
WHO CARE. . . .

A BEREAVEMENT SUPPORT GROUP

PURPOSE
The purpose of this monthly group is to provide emotional and spiritual support as well as practical, educational, and administrative assistance to people who are dealing with the loss of a loved one. Our goal is to assist each group member to cope with and recover from their personal loss so they can enjoy a balanced and fulfilled life.

EMOTIONAL SUPPORT
Monthly meetings are designed to provide a relaxed, accepting atmosphere for the fostering of friendships, healthy perspectives, group interaction, and practical input.

SPIRITUAL SUPPORT
It is also the intent of this support group to help each member recognize their great worth in the eyes of God. Short meditations will be shared at each meeting to enhance this goal. Weekly Bible studies will also be made available to support members who desire weekly meditations.

PRACTICAL ASSISTANCE
Transportation, domestic needs, errands, etc. are a part of the practical assistance offered by the support group.

EDUCATIONAL AND ADMINISTRATIVE ASSISTANCE
Monthly meetings will provide a variety of speakers, tapes, films, etc. dealing with issues related to bereavement. Literature dealing with the various aspects of bereavement will also be made available.

MEETING TIME AND PLACE
The bereavement support group will meet the third Monday evening of every month in the parlor at the Park Street Community Church from 7:00–8:30 P.M. (7:00–7:30—coffee and fellowship).

LOCATION
Park Street Community Church
999 Park Street
Middleville, Ohio 44805
Phone: 555-2222

(Insert map of location here)

Enter the education wing and look for signs.
The Parlor is located on the top floor, room 204.

Rear parking lot

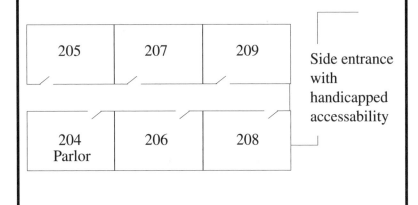

205	207	209
204 Parlor	206	208

Side entrance with handicapped accessability

WHEN DEATH HAS TOUCHED YOUR LIFE

THERE ARE PEOPLE WHO CARE. . . .

A BEREAVEMENT SUPPORT GROUP

PARK STREET COMMUNITY CHURCH
999 Park St., Middleville
For Information 555-2222
— Visitors Welcome —

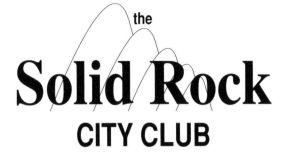

the

Solid Rock
CITY CLUB

MIDDLEVILLE, OHIO
AN EXCLUSIVE CLUB FOR SENIOR HIGH STUDENTS

DATE:	**FRIDAY, SEPT. 12TH**
LOCATION:	**MIDDLEVILLE YMCA**
TIME:	**8:00 – 11:00 P.M.**
ADMISSION:	**$1.00**

BASKETBALL

SOFT
DRINKS

VOLLEYBALL

MUSIC

FUTURE DATES: OCTOBER 8TH
NOVEMBER 12TH
DECEMBER 10TH

LIGHTS

FOOD

FUN

RELATED MATERIALS FOR RENEWAL THROUGH THE ADULT SUNDAY SCHOOL

3-A: Information Letter

Dear_____,

Thank you for agreeing to serve on the Sunday school growth task force! The focus of this task force is to examine carefully three goals—fellowship, outreach, and assimilation—in light of the past, present, and future. Following are working definitions of the three goals.

Fellowship: Informal gatherings of present and prospective class members for enjoyment, developing new friendships, and deepening existing ones.

Outreach: Building relationship bridges with persons outside of the Sunday school class with the express purpose of assimilating them into the class. Class members should be sensitive to the spiritual state of new attendees and should cultivate opportunities to share their personal faith in Christ, through word and deed, with any who are not Christians.

Assimilation: Integrating a new person into the social structure of a Sunday school class. Assimilation is only accomplished when the new person feels that he or she belongs.

The results of our examination will be specific ideas for further implementing these three foundational goals through our adult classes.

Overview of Task-Force Plan

Session 1: Past
In the history of your affiliation with this church, what have been some effective ways you have observed that have promoted fellowship, outreach, and assimilation in the adult Sunday school?

Session 2: Present
Based on effective past methods, as well as new insights suggested through group discussion and interviews with other members of your class, suggest effective strategies being used today.

Session 3: Future
Of the strategies suggested, which do you believe would be the most effective in your class? Propose a nine-month strategy including fellowship, outreach, and assimilation goals. Discuss this strategy with your class teacher, class president, and two other class members for their feedback.

Session 4: Implementation
Report to the group the results of your previous assignment and your specific goals. Work these through carefully with your teacher prior to this meeting. Present your

nine-month plan to the group. Make plans for a follow-up meeting.

Meeting Agenda

7:00–7:20. Prayer and devotional meditation; discuss personal insights from preparation worksheets in small groups.

7:20–7:40. Reports from each group; insights recorded and discussed.

7:40–8:00. Reflection and wrap-up of insights suggested by the ideas presented.

I look forward to seeing you at our first session.

* * *

3-B: Preparation Worksheet 1

Please answer these questions before the first session and be prepared to share your insights with other task force members.

1. What have been some of the effective activities you have observed in your adult Sunday school class that have promoted *fellowship* among present and/or prospective class members?

2. What have been some of the effective strategies you have observed that have encouraged *outreach* through intentionally building relationship bridges with persons outside of the class (Christian and non-Christian) with the express purpose of evangelism and/or assimilating them into the class?

3.   List the effective strategies you have observed in your class that have successfully *assimilated* new persons into the social structure.

* * *

3-C: Preparation Worksheet 2

Start early! This assignment will require more time than the first one.

1.   Compile a list that contains all the effective past strategies of fellowship, outreach, and assimilation suggested by the members of the Sunday school growth task force.

2.   Select two members of your Sunday school class, in coordination with the other member(s) of your task-force team, to interview over the phone or in the home. Record the names of the two you will interview. Your interviews should cover these matters.

   A. Give an update concerning the Sunday school growth task force: what it is meant to accomplish and what was discussed during the first session (the first letter you received and Preparation Worksheet 1 provide helpful material).

   B. Read the assorted strategies suggested by the task force and ask the class members to evaluate and recommend what they believe would be most effective in their class. If none of the strategies appeal to them, allow them to suggest new ones.

3.   After you have conducted both interviews, meet with the other team member(s) to compile the information you have received. Sift through all the suggestions and evaluations—including your

own—and determine one fellowship, one outreach, and one assimilation strategy you believe will be effective with your class. Record the strategies and come prepared to present them at the next task force meeting.

One *fellowship* strategy that will be effective in my Sunday school class

One *outreach* strategy that will be effective in my Sunday school class

One *assimilation* strategy that will be effective in my Sunday school class

❋   ❋   ❋

3-D: Preparation Worksheet 3

You have three weeks for this assignment. Make an appointment with the other member(s) of your task force team to attend to the following business.

1. Review the *fellowship, outreach,* and *assimilation* strategies you suggested on Preparation Worksheet 2. Decide if you desire to recommend these strategies to the class, or if there are others that may be more effective. Make a decision on the strategies you intend to propose.

fellowship
outreach
assimilation

2. Develop a nine-month time line with specific dates for planned events that will accomplish the fellowship, outreach, and assimilation strategies.

3. Generate a list of class members who might be interested in assuming the responsibilities of hospitality coordinator (ministry guidelines attached). List also those who might assist the coordinator with his or her tasks. It will not be necessary to contact these people until after the next task force session.

4. Discuss the time line and related information with your class teacher and class president and with two other class members for their feedback. You may want to choose from candidates listed above. Record their feedback here and on the back.

✳ ✳ ✳

3-E: Ministry Guidelines—Hospitality Coordinator

Purpose

The hospitality coordinator leads in fulfilling the various fellowship, outreach, and assimilation strategies established for the Sunday school class.

Personnel

One coordinator is selected for each class, with sufficient hospitality committee assistants to fulfill the class strategies.

Procedure

Hospitality Coordinators will
• develop and coordinate regular fellowship events;

- follow-up visitors and absentees weekly;
- assign contacts of prospective attendees, through home visits whenever possible and by invitations to social and fellowship events, to members of the hospitality committee or to other class members;
- welcome and introduce new attendees;
- promote the regular fellowship events;
- perform other tasks deemed necessary to further fellowship, outreach, and assimilation.

Provisions

The church facilities will be available on a scheduled basis for fellowship events.

* * *

3-F: Preparation Worksheet 4

1. Contact the class members you recommended on Preparation Worksheet 3 as candidates for hospitality coordinator and the hospitality committee. Discuss with each person adequate background information, your proposed strategies, the nine-month time line, and where you see him or her fitting in. Continue making contacts until you have secured sufficient volunteers. Record the names of those who have *agreed* to be responsible for these positions.

   Hospitality coordinator

   Hospitality committee personnel

2. Establish a date (with your teacher's agreement) to present the nine-month time line, along with your

vision for growth, to the class. Allow time for class
discussion. Also invite the hospitality coordinator
and members of the hospitality committee to speak,
if they desire. Be sensitive to other members of the
class who may also desire to serve on the hospitality
committee.

Record the date you plan to share with your class

Record their response

3. Now we're off and running! The task force will meet
    in one month to discuss progress and any difficul-
    ties you may experience.
    The date of this meeting will be _____

4. On a separate page, please record your evaluations,
    pro and con, of the four Sunday school growth task
    force sessions.

    *Note: Please provide the pastor with the names of
    persons on the hospitality committee.*

3-G: Visitation Form

Dear [hospitality coordinator],
Thank you for visiting new contacts on behalf of your
Sunday school class. Please make a personal visit in this
home sometime in the next three weeks.
Names of all in home and approximate ages of children

Vocation(s)

Address/phone

Directions to the home

Date of pastor's visit

Staff person who visited

Other information

Please call prior to your visit to establish a convenient time. The enclosed postcard can be completed and mailed to the church office following your visit. This card will help us keep track of each call made.

Thanks so much for participating in this vital ministry.

*   *   *

3-H: Preparation Worksheet 5

Meet with the teacher, the hospitality coordinator, the task-force team for your class, and the hospitality committee members to discuss these matters.

1. Evaluate the *fellowship*, *outreach*, and *assimilation* strategies utilized over the past year. Decide which strategies require revision and which are effective. Dialogue until the group forms a consensus concerning the fellowship, outreach, and assimilation strategies for the coming year.

   fellowship
   outreach
   assimilation

2. Develop a nine-month time line of dates for planned events to fulfill these strategies.

3. The hospitality coordinator and hospitality committee members should indicate their commitment
to continue their responsibilities for the coming
year. If additional or replacement personnel are
needed, create a list of class members who might
be interested in assuming the responsibilities. The
names, along with the person(s) responsible to contact each, can be recorded here.

*Note: It will not be necessary to contact these people
until after the next session.*